What did Jesus tell us about happiness? Did He promise a success formula or prosperity formula? Did He tell us that it would be provided by a family member? He says happiness comes for those who are poor in spirit, mourn, are gentle, desire to be righteous, are merciful, have pure desires, make peace, and are persecuted because of their righteousness.

What Jesus is saying is this: Happiness does not come from other people causing us to be happy, nor by their doing things for us. It does not come by having more, doing more, dominating others, or by getting our own way. It comes from inside of us and is reflected by relating to others with a sense of openness, concern and humility.

HOW TO TREAT YOUR FAMILY

AS WELL AS YOU TREAT YOUR

FRIENDS

Judson J. Swihart

Regal Books

A Division of GL Publications
Ventura, CA U.S.A.

Rights for publishing this book in other languages are contracted by Gospel Literature International foundation (GLINT). GLINT also provides technical help for the adaptation, translation, and publishing of Bible study resources and books in more than 100 languages worldwide. For further information, contact GLINT, Post Office Box 6688, Ventura, California 93006, U.S.A., or the publisher.

Scripture quotations in this publication are primarily paraphrased by the author. Exact quotes are from *The New King James Bible*, New Testament. Copyright © 1979, Thomas Nelson, Inc., Publishers.

Second Printing, 1985

Published by Regal Books
A Division of GL Publications
Ventura, California 93006
Printed in U.S.A.

Library of Congress Cataloging in Publication Data
Swihart, Judson J.
    How to treat your family as well as you treat your friends.

    1. Marriage.   2. Interpersonal relations.
3. Family—Religious life.   4. Marriage—Religious
aspects—Christianity.   I. Title
HQ734.S984   1982   646.7'8   82-11234
ISBN 0-8307-0855-3

Contents

I would like to dedicate this book to my parents, Marjorie and Noble Swihart. They are the ones who laid the foundation in my life that has allowed me to grow to an awareness of the Kingdom Life. I have often wondered where I would be in life if I had not had their influence in the construction of faith.

I would like to express my deep appreciation to Dallas Willard and Gordon Mollett who taught and directed me to think about the Kingdom of God, and to the many friends who talked, questioned and encouraged me in my thinking.

I would also like to thank Pat Hayes for her helpful thinking about the manuscript and her typing, and Sandra Worcester who typed the final draft.

Introduction

They had been married for nine years. It had not always been easy. They had come through many struggles and some had left scars that would take time to heal. Things were better now. They did not argue so much. They knew each other more deeply and had a respect for each other. Essentially, they had both come into the marriage with some needs left over from childhood.

He was the older of two brothers, reared by a father who worked hard and who was seldom able to talk about his feelings. His mother had been quite controlling, so he was edgy about another woman in his life telling him what to do.

She was a middle child. Her father had left her mother when she was five. He visited her every other weekend for the first couple of years, and then the visits faded away. Now she seldom hears from her father. Coming into marriage she wondered if all men were likely to ignore her needs.

Now, nine years later, they were still the same

people. Their families hadn't changed. They had changed somewhat—but not much. So why was their marriage better?

I find that often Christians have a desire to know and understand what the Bible teaches about marriage and family relationships. We want to know sometimes for good reasons—such as a desire for a strong Christian marriage or concern about being a better spouse or parent. Sometimes we want to know for less valid reasons—such as to relieve guilt over the way we are relating; or we want to find a verse we can use as a tool to pressure our spouse into changing, or to show the spouse just how wrong he is behaving.

When people desire to look into the Scriptures to search what the Bible teaches on marriage, they turn to Ephesians 5 and 6, 1 Corinthians 7, and 1 Peter 3. Their next step is to take a good concordance and look up passages that focus on words like marriage, husband, wife, family, children, etc. Or they purchase Christian books having to do with marriage, most of which address these same passages.

This type of searching assumes that what the Bible has to say about marriage and family is taught *only* when these specific terms are used. However, I believe that Christ taught many principles about relating to other people that should apply in our homes first of all. Spouses and children do not carry exclusion clauses. For example, is it not reasonable to conclude that when Christ teaches us how to interact with others, we would apply the teaching to our family relationships first since, hopefully, these are the people we interact with the most? Yet why is it that we treat people we see for an hour on Sunday better than our own families? Is it not a mistake to assume that the passage does not apply to families since the passage of Scripture does not use a key word such as *marriage* or *children*? To compartmentalize the teachings of the Bible in such a fashion does not give us a full perspective of what the Bible does teach about marriage and family relationships. When we delete passages on relationships because they do not use key words or phrases, we can jump to the conclusion that much of the Bible's teachings on marriage have to do with role relationships and a set of rules on when to marry (or when one can get out of a marriage) and still be in God's will. By a review of Christian literature we can see where there are many different opinions about these matters and much sincere debate over just how and when these rules apply and don't apply.

Many times I have sat in my office with individuals and couples, who, after reading several Christian books on marriage, were trying to untangle the web of confusion caused by the conflicting perspectives of sincere and well-educated authors. I am not proposing that we ignore these teachings on marriage or family, for I feel they are valuable and exist for the purpose of our edification. I think to discount them would also be a mistake. However, I believe that we lose much by narrowing our understanding of marriage and family to these few passages of Scripture. We need to seek to understand what these teach us about relating, but we also need to look beyond them to focus on other passages that have to do with relating to others, applying the principles to our family through the ebb and flow of everyday life. When the kids throw a football across the living room and break a lamp, or the husband comes home angry at his wife for

being cold and indifferent to him during breakfast, what is needed is guidance about relating to
others, not principles of submission, or who is the
head of the family.

When our focus is only on role relationship,
there is a danger of drifting toward legalism to the
exclusion of having a right heart. Was this not the
frequent conflict that Christ had with the Pharisees? They did the right things for the wrong reasons. Christ described them as "whitewashed
tombs" (Matt. 23:27) and told His followers that
unless their righteousness surpassed that of the
Pharisees they would not enter the kingdom of
heaven (Matt. 5:20). Sure, they gave to the church,
prayed in public, and followed the law; yet Christ
was more interested in what was going on in their
hearts and how they treated other people, as He
goes on to describe in the verses following Matthew 5:20. In the remainder of the chapter He tells
them what the law says and contrasts that with
what He says.

In a similar vein, we need to broaden our
understanding of relationships so that in our families we are not like the Pharisees, doing all the
right things, but with the wrong motivation
inside. God has called us to a sense of freedom in
our relationships, not a sense of more rules by
which we can earn our salvation. When rules
become the main way of relating to God, guilt cannot be far behind. Often we see those who are
loaded down with the weight of trying to fulfill the
rules to the point that they miss out on the joy of
relationships. We need to have principles while
simultaneously experiencing the freedom of our
faith. ("You are free indeed," see John 8:36.)

In summary, then, my concern is that we study

the Scriptures having to do specifically with marriage and family, but that we do not stop at that point. We need to go further and seek to understand how the teachings of Christ apply to the way we treat our spouse and children in everyday life. Therefore, in the following chapters, I would like to present what I believe Christ taught about relationships in the Sermon on the Mount in Matthew 5—7 and how I believe these teachings apply in families. I find this study fascinating because these teachings consistently go 180 degrees against that which we are taught by the world and that which we think we know. These teachings flow against the current of our human nature, as we shall see when we study such aspects as "don't return evil for evil" or "love your enemy."

These teachings in Matthew are not only radically exciting but they seem to me to be the central point of the whole New Testament. Sometimes I wonder if much of Paul's teachings in the New Testament needed to have been written if the early church had applied Jesus' teachings to their lives. For example, it seems to me that much of Paul's admonitions came as a result of people *not* living the Kingdom Life that Christ taught. What Christ teaches is difficult to apply and sounds very idealistic. It is idealistic, in fact, and very different from the kind of life we live in our family relationships and the philosophies we assimilate in our world. We are told to not be conformed to the world, and when we look at relationships as Christ taught them, we can see the contrast. Life in the fast lane does not look like that described in Matthew 5.

In looking at the ideal in Matthew, I am not optimistic enough to think that people will ever live according to His principles 100 percent or even 75 percent of the time. As my family could tell you, even though I have as my personal goal a Kingdom Life, I have a long way to go before living there consistently. I agree with Dr. Henry Brandt and Phil Landrum in their book *I Want My Marriage to Be Better* when they state that "we all have a human nature and a drive toward selfishness, stubbornness, deception, etc. Marriages do not make us this way; it's just that our natures come to the surface around those with whom we live."[1] It seems to me that what our families do for us is to provide convenient people on whom to blame our old natures so that we don't have to be responsible for our feelings and our actions. As I recall, some other people like Adam and Eve had a similar problem.

"I am really in a bad mood lately because my husband has been drinking again." "She makes me so mad, because of the way she ignores my needs." "The kids are absolutely driving me crazy—I just have to watch TV soap operas in the afternoon to keep my sanity."

Whatever feelings we have we can always find somebody else in the family that caused them. Part of the tragedy of this is that we cannot resolve our feelings until we own them. As long as you make me angry, I don't have to do a thing—you're the one who has to change. So, as it often goes, others are viewed as the reason for behaviors we don't wish to own. Yet, in Christ's teachings in Matthew we are taught to accept personal responsibility for radically different behavior and attitudes.

In an era of family dysfunction, we need to refocus on what Christ said and to consider how His teachings apply to our lives in our homes today.

Even if our marriages and families are self-defeating, we can find life and vitality that we never dreamed possible when we live the Kingdom Life. This is partly what Jesus meant when He said, "I am come that you might have life and have it more abundantly" (see John 10:10).

When Jesus teaches, He is talking about what it means to live in the Kingdom. What I am presenting here for your consideration is not a set of rules by which you should attempt to live. To make more rules by which to live and judge others goes against the Kingdom Life itself. What I am describing is what family life can be when people's responses to each other are an outgrowth of living in the Kingdom. For us to take these principles as a set of rigid rules by which to live would only produce a sense of frustration and perhaps some guilt as we fail.

I want to share principles which, when followed, will release the potential vitality and freedom that families can have. I see Christ's teachings as shining hope in an era that has not been laden with optimism for the family. The ways of life advocated by society have not produced as they promised. Following these principles from the Sermon on the Mount can bring the fulfillment that hasn't always been there.

Questions for Discussion

1. Do you agree or disagree that Christ's teachings in Matthew have their strongest application to the family relationship?

2. Why is it so difficult to treat our own family members as well as we treat others?

3. In what ways do you see people in the family doing the right behavior but with the wrong

motives? In what way is this like the righteousness of the Pharisees?

4. What difference can you see in the lives of those people who have a sense of freedom in their relationships compared to those whose relationships are governed by rules?

5. In what ways could the teachings of Christ have a negative effect if you make them into a new set of rules by which to live?

Note
1. Henry Brandt and Phil Landrum, *I Want My Marriage to Be Better* (Grand Rapids: Zondervan Publishing House, 1976).

Matthew 5:1-12

And seeing the multitudes, He went up on a mountain, and when He was seated His disciples came to Him. And He opened His mouth and taught them, saying:

"Blessed are the poor in spirit, for theirs is the kingdom of heaven.

"Blessed are those who mourn, for they shall be comforted.

"Blessed are the gentle, for they shall inherit the earth.

"Blessed are those who hunger and thirst for righteousness, for they shall be filled.

"Blessed are the merciful, for they shall obtain mercy.

"Blessed are the pure in heart, for they shall see God.

"Blessed are the peacemakers, for they shall be called the sons of God.

"Blessed are those who are persecuted for righteousness' sake, for theirs is the kingdom of heaven.

"Blessed are you when they revile and persecute you, and say all manner of evil against you falsely for My sake.

"Rejoice and be exceedingly glad, for great is your reward in heaven, for so they persecuted the prophets who were before you."

1

Living Happily

Matthew 5:1-12

In Matthew, as Christ starts His ministry, He sends shock waves through His society that are still shaking our society. He makes explicit and direct statements about life that contradict our whole way of living and being. Many times we find His teachings too out of our realm of thinking to consider serious application. We have trouble relating to that which we have not seen in our own life experience. Yet, it is through these applications that one can find life with all its fullness.

In the Sermon on the Mount Christ starts out with the "who are the happy" list. These we call the Beatitudes. Most translations use the word "blessed" but a more contemporary translation would be "happy." As I look at the list, I too find it in stark contrast to what society says makes people happy. We are taught that in our society and family we should achieve happiness by getting the things we want, getting people to treat us well, being successful in what we try to achieve. In families, people become focused on whether or not they are being treated fairly. They want happiness and feel that it is owed to them from their families, jobs, and environment.

Many husbands and wives hold each other responsible for their happiness. They go into the marriage with high expectations of all the wonderful things they will get out of this new institution they are about to enter. He anticipates that she will get up looking like a queen, make his breakfast, be delighted in all he has to share with her about his hobby and the boys at the shop.

One morning she gets up tired, her hair in curlers, could care less about his new fishing reel, and is complaining about his not getting the bills paid. He now faces a crisis of relationship. After all, doesn't she want him to be happy? If so, why does she treat him so badly? He is now unhappy and it is her fault because she makes him that way. He doesn't have to change—she does. Therefore, just as soon as she shapes up he can start being happy again. Now his newfound task becomes that of shaping her up, because he really would like to be happy again. In his own mind he has relinquished the responsibility to her for his feelings—in this case, feelings of happiness.

People come into marriage expecting it to fulfill some of the gaps from childhood. When we find the spouse is not the all-nurturing, all-omnipotent parent we always believed would bring everlasting happiness, we are amazed. The first marital shock is finding that the angel we married is not an immortal but a human being with her own needs.

What did Jesus tell us about happiness? Did He promise a success formula or prosperity formula? Did He tell us that it would be provided by a family member? He says those who are poor in spirit, mourn, are gentle, desire to be righteous, are merciful, have pure desires, make peace, and are persecuted because of their righteousness are going to be happy.

How can this be? Are we not taught that those who push hard to get ahead find happiness in the process? Are not those who have such strong personalities that they can out-argue others to get their own way, happier because of it? Shouldn't you outmaneuver others so they won't take advantage of you? Suppose your teenager doesn't deserve any mercy for the low grade on the last test. Don't you have the obligation as the parent to really let him have it with both barrels so he won't do it again? Shouldn't you as the father work 14 hours a day so the family can have more and do more and be happy? After all, the Smiths just got a new boat that makes your boat look tacky.

What Jesus is saying is this: Happiness does not come from other people causing us to be happy, nor by their doing things for us. It does not come by having more, doing more, dominating others, or by getting our own way. It comes from inside of us and is reflected by relating to others with a sense of openness, concern and humility.

Dr. John MacArthur, Jr. precisely states it by saying that in Jesus' first sermon, the stress is on "being," not ruling or possessing. There is a whole new world on the inside that reflects itself by the way we relate to God and treat others on the outside.[1] There is great emphasis on the way we are, not only on our following all the rules. William Jordan, in *Marriage: A Discovery Together*, defines happiness as a paradox revealed by the depth of inner life that consists of being, not having and enjoying, not possessing. "It is a heart at peace with itself."[2]

As we will see, Jesus goes on to tell the disciples that their righteousness needs to exceed that of the Pharisees who were trying to do all the right things, but inside their hearts were not right. As a result they became puffed up, self-elevating; they judged others and looked down on them. They were model citizens, but were they gentle with other people? Were they merciful with others? Did they have pure motivation for relating to others? Or did they manipulate and set traps in order to put someone down and make him look foolish?

What happens in families that they are not functioning well? Emotionally, people are bullied, possessed, used, manipulated, ignored and/or despised. They may well be held accountable for others' happiness. We are taught a new lesson in the Beatitudes—that we will never achieve that elusive happiness by these styles of interaction. I believe that the characteristic, which Jesus taught was associated with happiness, was that of spiritual rightness that is reflected in the way we treat others.

This, then, is seen as a spiritual principle that is expressed from God through us to others. Those who have received mercy have the strength to show mercy to others; those whose hearts have been cleansed and are pure relate to others with a pure heart rather than with manipulation. Therefore, happy are those who are peacemakers for two reasons: First, they are happy because they have received the peace of God; secondly, they are happy because peaceable relationships with others are the most fulfilling way of life emotionally.

The Beatitudes are focused on two relationships—man's relationship to God and man's relationship to others. Happy is the person who hungers for righteousness—man's relationship to God. Happy is the person who is meek, merciful, gentle, a peacemaker—man's relationship to others.

The more I have considered the Sermon on the Mount in conjunction with the rest of the Scripture, the more clear it becomes that when our relationship with God is what He wants it to be, it will have a tremendous and direct impact on the way we treat others, particularly our own families. In fact, it seems to me that most of the sins that are listed in the Bible come back to this sermon and are an abridgement of how we are taught to live. Lying, stealing, committing adultery, gossiping, backbiting, coveting, envying, hating, being jealous, not caring for the poor, widows or orphans, etc.—are not all of these a list of products that come from not following the teachings of this sermon? Are not all of these involving the way we treat other people? I conclude then that much of sin is against God but involves the way we treat others.

There are two considerations in the application of the Beatitudes. Is this list of those who are happy stating that if you are doing these things you will become happy? Or is it saying that if you are happy you will be relating to God and others in this manner? Which comes first—the chicken or the egg? Perhaps, in this case, there is a circular relationship taking place in which these ways of living both cause happiness and are a product of happiness.

The second consideration of the Beatitudes has to do with whether these are spiritual principles or emotional principles or some combination of the two. Although there is a difference of opinion by some scholars, I believe the principles are both spiritual and emotional. For example, "Happy are those who mourn, for they shall be comforted" (see Matt. 5:4) may well apply to mourning about one's sin; however, I also realize that a person who allows himself to be open emotionally so that his grief is shared with others who can comfort him, also finds happiness. Perhaps these are not mutually exclusive so that they have to be categorized as either spiritual or emotional principles. Perhaps they are principles that have spiritual *and* emotional application.

They had it made. He had his business in addition to his corporate executive position. He had pushed hard for years and had climbed well up the executive ladder. One look at his clothes and you knew he was important. His manner was that of self-assurance. He told his fellow workers how to run the show and was verbally skilled and aggressive in meetings. She had a large home, new car, clothes and all the right friends around town. She was active, knew what she wanted and was socially skilled. Their kids were class officers and on the sports teams.

They had been married for 18 years, most of which had been the longest, most critical war on record. He would blame her for his misery and try to force her to change. She blamed him for their problems and refused to cooperate with his demands. She screamed; he yelled; both called each other names. Neither would ever admit to being wrong or having wronged the other. Sometimes he would add pressure by becoming ill and making her feel guilty, at which time she would give in—only to get back at him the next day with a counterpunch of overspending. Their marriage consisted of many threats, separations, and a constant discussion of divorcing each other.

They stood their ground, were never wrong—happy are the meek.

They lashed at each other with hostility—happy are the gentle.

Their lives centered on prosperity, status, popularity—happy are those who hunger for righteousness.

They manipulated each other with guilt—happy are the pure in heart.

They attacked and counterattacked often and viciously—happy are the peacemakers.

For years they sought happiness and relief but never seemed to be able to find it. "We can't keep going on like this. There must be more out there. We are no different now than we were ten years ago." On and on they pressed, and at my last contact with them they were still looking.

Most families have similar situations but not always with the constant battling of this family. How do the Beatitudes apply? Every day, when a couple comes together or mother interacts with daughter, the same issues are there. Does that husband have a humble spirit or a superior attitude? Does the mother treat the child with respect or disdain? Does each take his role in the family and use it with humility or use it to bring pressure on other family members to make them bend under the pressure? "As the head of this family, I make the decisions—your ideas are neither wanted, nor valued, nor accepted—I know what I'm doing." Hardly like the King of kings refusing to pull rank on those coming to arrest Him.

Poor in Spirit

What constitutes poverty? Is it not primarily being without self-sufficiency? A person with a poor spirit is one who realizes that he is not a self-contained, totally self-sufficient unit. He realizes this both spiritually and emotionally. This person is humbled by the awareness of who he is before God and by his ability to be good as well as evil. He does not think he is Mr. Wonderful or Miss Superiority. He has a sense of his relatedness to God as well as his need for relationships with those around him.

For the person struggling to be somebody, to be rich in power, and able to lord it over others, this is quite a startling sermon lead. Christ says, "It's those who are poor in spirit who can find happiness" (see Matt. 5:3). What about all the books on looking out for number one, or on effective intimidation that promises to lead one to success and happiness? Then there is the person who is loaded with pride because he is the most humble person he knows. What about his happiness?

There are also those people who appear to be poor in spirit mainly because they have zero self-acceptance. They look humble enough, but it is not because they have never dealt with the issue of humility.

The group Christ was addressing was not the up and outers, but the everyday people. He was saying *they* could be happy too. Happiness was not reserved exclusively for the Pharisees.

I look at families to find those who relate to each other out of a poor spirit. Things have been tight financially. Faced with cold fall weather you

scrape together the money to buy Todd that new
jacket he needs. A week later he comes home without it. He took if off to play football after school and
just forgot it. Does Dad talk to his son from the
position of a poor spirit?

She has been really critical of her husband all
week. She is displeased with everything he has
done. He has been quietly brooding inside, storing
up his resentment at her little digs. Will he be able
to tell her his feelings from a position of "poor in
spirit"? Or will he unload with all the force of
Mount Vesuvius?

Mourning

"Happy are those who mourn" (Matt. 5:4)
seems very incongruent at first glance. How can
someone who is mourning be happy? The point
here is that the happiness may follow the mourning, rather than taking place simultaneously. It is
when a person is comforted that he feels happiness. Without first mourning, he can experience
no comfort.

Society tries to run on a constant high. It pur-
sues a constant state of happiness, thrill, pleasure, or excitement. This perhaps gets out of balance. To think you can be happy only by the
pursuit of fulfillment is erroneous. There is a season for those things, but there is also a season for
sadness. People will go to great lengths to avoid
any pain in their lives that could lead to mourning. They use denial, avoidance, postponement,
substitution or over-involvement to avoid it. In so
doing, they deprive themselves of a meaningful
part of life and the rich feelings that come from
allowing themselves to receive the comfort others
can give.

They had been married for seven years. Part of the time Barbara had found enjoyment; other times the relationship had been empty. Mike had not wanted the divorce but she was not to be deterred. She wanted more emotional input than she felt from him. She wanted it desperately because she had not felt it from her father either. Mike was a strong person and he showed it through the divorce process. He didn't need her, although he did sometimes talk about missing the kids. He soon was busy with his work, putting in more hours than ever—some weeks 60 or 70 hours. He hardly had time for the kids anymore because he was also on the church softball team and taking care of his own shopping, laundry, and apartment. He never dealt with his hurt and sense of loss. He was too busy. It was only a couple of years later while in counseling that he got in touch with his grief over the loss of Barbara. Then he could mourn and be comforted. It was then he found resolution and healing. It was then the depression lifted and joy returned again to his life. Happy are those who mourn.

Certainly the spiritual application is also very visible to those who look. The person who never deals with the issue of sin in his life and his need for reconciliation to God will never experience the comfort of forgiveness. To deny this need does not mean the need magically disappears. Once the Comforter has done His job, certainly with our thanksgiving, happiness rises like the morning sun.

Gentleness/Meekness
How can someone who is gentle or meek be

happy? (See Matt. 5:5.) Doesn't he get trampled under by herds of assertive people who are out there charging like buffalo? Meek people are also blessed and happy. Perhaps we have some false images of what Christ meant by meek. I do not think He was talking about a person who relates to others like a flashlight with a weak battery. Meekness needs to come from a position of strength, not weakness. One having the ability to push for his position and yet choosing to allow others to do it their way is a more accurate picture. You have met people who you felt had a sense of powerlessness. How do you treat them? Does happiness emanate from outdoing or overpowering other people who may not be as strong as you?

The conflict in families is certainly not coming from people being overly meek. Power struggles exist on all levels. Our behavior is just the opposite of what Christ taught. He tries to force her into getting a new four-wheel. She wants a family car. The daughter is not about to give up seeing the boy her parents dislike and takes her stand. She will show them—they can't make her give him up; she confronts them by seeing him after school or ditching with him for the day.

Hungry and Thirsty

Happy are those who have an insatiable appetite for righteousness (see Matt. 5:6). In my family, as the older children approach adolescence, I am learning about appetites. The kids are constantly munching on something or standing in front of the refrigerator with the door open. Reflect on the past week. For what have you hungered? Companionship? Attention? Power? A right relationship with God? How did you spend your time and what does that say about your appetite?

It's difficult to have a right relationship with God, one that is free from guilt and sin, without having right relationships in our families. Every day we are confronted with opportunities to treat other family members in ways that are more right than others.

Some people go through life like a bull in a china shop. They are insensitive to the damage they can cause in the lives of those closest to them. They are oblivious to the impact they have in their interactions with others, and they often cause unnecessary pain. On the other hand, those who are hungry for right relationships with God and in their families choose to treat others in ways that are in accordance with God's will. These ways may be more demanding of time and energy and may even require self-sacrifice, but they are right. In this passage we are taught that happiness comes from hungering and thirsting for righteousness. In the coming chapters we will consider some of Jesus' teaching on right ways to treat others.

Mercy

The concept of showing mercy in a family is one I seldom see taught. In fact, I know of no book designed to encourage and teach family members how to treat each other better with mercy. Isn't it interesting that we live in a society with a proliferation of books on how to meet all your own needs but with virtually nothing on how to show more mercy?

In families you focus on personal rights and the concept of fairness. Both of these lead you away from showing mercy to one another. Mercy means giving help to relieve the suffering or pain of another even when it involves giving of yourself in a way that may not be fair to you.

Mercy involves many aspects of not exploiting another person at a time when he is helpless in meeting his own needs. Within the family context, this also means not stepping on the other individual at a point of his personal weakness. For it is within the family that each member's weaknesses become obvious to the others. Our human nature seems to tell us that when we are impacted by the weakness of another family member, we should strike back hard so that person will learn not to be weak in that way or because that person has interfered in our life. Yet, when we look at the mercy shown by God, we can only be grateful that He introduced this concept of mercy into the world.

This concept results in Kingdom living. Sometimes the church falls short—it teaches kids to not smoke pot and to stay out of porno theaters, but forgets to teach them the importance of showing mercy.

Mercy means helping at a time of need and can be conveyed by the way the help is offered as well as by the act itself. Interestingly, mercy cannot be shown to anyone other than at a point of need. How can you show mercy to someone when everything is going his way? Perhaps, since mercy does involve some sense of helplessness on the part of the other person, the difficulty in expressing it comes from being at a point where you are in control. You could lord it over the other person but are faced with the choice not to do so. Of course, this then means showing mercy, not in a condescending fashion, but with humility and concern. This showing of mercy goes against our old human nature. It is clear from reading Romans 1, which describes society, that unmercifulness is the antithesis of living in the Kingdom. After listing unrighteousness, greed, inventing evil—along with many other characteristics, Paul concludes with "unmerciful."

Perhaps your son has had a day at school when he felt nothing went right. He had not done his math homework so he had to face the consequences, which included some personal embarrassment in front of his class. He comes home to mow the lawn. Being preoccupied about his day at school, he runs the mower over the garden hose and slices it. How will you treat him? Is this a time to ready yourself for a half-hour lecture, or a time for mercy?

Does a parent unload his own frustration and anger at having to replace the hose or does he see a person who is already hurting and trying to regain his emotional footing? Certainly this situation is complex. There are many issues involved, such as bearing consequences of behavior, handling disappointments, teaching responsibility, teaching concentration on a task. However, teaching children to show mercy is best done through their experiencing it, perhaps even in situations where they deserve it least. It is my observation, however, that most of the time when parents are dealing with their children, rarely is mercy even one of the options considered.

He came home from work late. She had decided to hold dinner until he arrived. Now dinner was cold. Her hard work and careful preparation were virtually wiped out by his lack of consideration. Her disappointment was great and her frustration high. "Where have you been? I've been waiting an hour. The kids are starving. I work my head off around here trying to prepare a decent meal and you don't even bother to show up for dinner, let alone call. They do have an invention these days called a telephone, you know"—on and on she drones with subtle and not so subtle condemnations and humiliations prior to finding out why he was late. Happy are those who show mercy.

Pure Heart

"Pure in heart" (see Matt. 5:8) implies that someone has gone through some type of cleansing or purifying process so that on the inside he will be clean and, therefore, relate to others from a position of pure motives. This Beatitude tells us that we will see God, in the sense of understanding God's purity.

A pure heart is reflected in families by relating to others with pure motives. The wife decides she is going to make those scalloped potatoes for him tonight because he really loves them. She is not preparing him for the idea that she has bought a new dress. She is not warding off his anger from their spat at breakfast. She is not proving to him her worth by trying to be a great cook. She is not even trying to elicit a loving response. She is doing something she wants to do in order to express her love.

It could be fascinating to see a research study designed to measure the percent of hidden agendas families have for every 100 interactions between them. Many interactions are designed to gain our own way, make the other person feel less adequate, prove our worth, gain something that we feel we cannot ask for directly, or deceive. The reasons people choose to interact are not always pure but often manipulative or self-centered.

She feared that nobody would really care for her. Her husband had moved out several years earlier and ever since, underneath the surface, she basically did not trust men. She never planned to remarry. She had several sons and began the process of binding them to her. They were often made to feel responsible for her. She would ask them to help her with tasks she could have done herself. They were discouraged from having friends, especially girl friends. They were indulged and had every need cared for so they grew dependent. No one could fault a mother for loving her kids so much that she cared for them so well. As adults, two of them found themselves still living at home. Finally, the older one moved out and the younger son ended up being left behind with full care of his mother. He often thought of leaving, but could always find logical reasons for not doing so.

The results of relating out of an unpure heart are usually destructive either to the personhood of the recipient or to the relationship itself. Either way they ultimately affect the person with the lack of pure motives. Observing these kinds of relationships makes it clear that it is what comes out of a person that brings defilement.

Peacemakers

One of the signs of being followers of Christ's teachings is that we become peacemakers. In your own family do people think of you as a peacemaker? The idea of being a peacemaker stirs up many concepts of how to behave toward people, some of which I think do not actually lead to peace. A sense

of peace comes from harmony or a sense of reconciliation. This includes harmony within the person and in relationship to other family members.
The only road to harmony is to take that which is
divergent and bring it to a point of merger. When
we talk of peace within we think in terms of con-
gruences, not identicalness. This is what we see
happening when we bring our spiritual maladies
to God and find reconciliation with Him by His
provision for them through Christ. Then a peace
which is different from that found in the world is
formed in us. We come from a point of divergence
with God to a point of reconciliation.

Being a peacemaker does not come about by
avoiding divergence or conflict. It does not come
about by trying to overlook differences of opinion.
And it certainly does not entail taking one's angry
feelings and pushing them inside. A peacemaker
in a family deals with issues, but for the peacemaker the focus is on a reconciled relationship. He
does not constantly strive to win—winning is the
goal of battles and wars. He does strive for reconciliation.

Bill and Sue wanted a Christian marriage. He
wanted to be loving and kind—a peaceable person.
Often he called her darling or honey in the daily
routine of life. At times she was critical of him.
Inside he would feel pain similar to the pain he
had received in the barrage of nonacceptance he
had experienced as a child. On those occasions he
would push aside his feelings, put on his best
smile and voice and overlook her comments. He
was a peacemaker in their relationship. Inside
there was no peace; he was furious. And then peri-
odically the dam would break and the anger would

come flooding out. Furthermore, he began keeping mental I.O.U.'s. In his eyes, she became deeply indebted to him for all the times he had overlooked their differences. Many years after they said their "I do's" he found himself isolated from her. He didn't care much any more. Inside he longed to leave her but he could never say that, since neither he nor the church believed in divorce. He stayed, but the resentment finally faded into indifference.

Being a peacemaker means getting to the issues—not avoiding them. It means that husbands and wives should express their differences and their feelings of hurt and anger. As David Augsburger expresses, it means "caring enough to confront."[3] However heated it becomes, the movement of the discussion is always with the purpose of reconciliation. We have an excellent example of the importance of reconciliation a few verses later, in Matthew 5:23 and 24, where Christ gives instruction to people who are about to worship. When they remember that their brother is upset at them, they are to go and be reconciled first and then come and worship. In this case, it is not the peacemaker who is the distressed party, yet he is still required to reach out to make peace. If reconciliation takes precedence over worship in Christ's teachings, is not being a peacemaker important?

Reconciliation is also seen in the way God was willing to reach out and make peace with man in his state of spiritual distress. Woven through Scripture is this constant thread of God's desire to see mankind reconciled to Him. In the family, where there is an opportunity to live out and reflect this characteristic of God, people often prefer others to be the initiators of peace. So often people do not want to reach out, but feel that because they have been offended, their spouse or child should be the one who comes to them—preferably hat in hand.

Being a peacemaker seems to be more an active role than a passive role. It means initiating rather than waiting or ignoring. The development of attitudes that lead to peacemaking can be started by the way in which parents intervene in the conflicts of their children. When the kids get into a dispute it is important to not ignore their quarrel (except in cases where parents deliberately do so to allow their children to develop the skills to resolve it). It is likewise important to not deal merely with the issue of the dispute by rendering a judgment such as, "I clearly remember it is Billy's turn to wash the dishes." Parents also need to encourage the children to reconcile their own relationship. Parents need to encourage healing of any pain they experience in a conflict. In this training, a child develops the concept of dealing with relating to others as well as with issues.

A family of peacemakers certainly would be a lot more fun to live in than a family with constant turbulence. A family may want to become more like our poster scene of the lion lying down with the lamb. This means that each member must initiate peacemaking rather than waiting for the others to change in some way. You usually think of your spouse as being the lion with you as the lamb, and you will have peace as soon as he/she changes. A peacemaker needs to be the initiator rather than a waiter on lions.

Suffering

Happy are those who suffer in some way as a result of their obedience to what God wants them to do. This seems really to be the summary of the last two Beatitudes.

On a spiritual plane we can realize that, since the people of the world have always rejected the righteousness of God, they will likewise be distressed, puzzled, and frustrated when they see a person living in a way that reflects Christ. This passage addresses itself to an issue that we have trouble understanding in depth because, at this point in history, there is little suffering on the part of American Christians as a result of their faith. We can only relate to some sense of humiliation or being laughed at, as opposed to the martyrdom of the early church. Seen in context with the rest of chapter 5, "happy are those who suffer" emphasizes again the importance of living in the Kingdom in such a manner that all other aspects of life lose their importance.

On a lesser plane, there is also the suffering that comes from rejecting the world's value system. The Beatitudes encourage humility; being a peacemaker, not a winner of battles; showing mercy rather than exploiting for personal gain. When a person does these things he is looked down on by those who have it all going for them and are surfing across the sea of life.

In a family, a person must make decisions daily about how he is going to handle various situations. In the process of living the Kingdom Life, he will give up some experiences, such as the triumph of winning a battle over the spouse who is emotionally backed into a corner; or he may not be able to release his feelings of frustration toward a child by really letting the child have it.

She was married to a nonbelieving husband

who suffered form some severe struggles due to an emotionally hostile childhood environment, as well as post-Vietnam delayed stress reactions. He was often verbally abusive to her and emotionally pushed her away from a feeling of closeness to him. He vacillated between closeness and distance. Every time they got close, he predictably would do something to create more distance. He would often spend his Saturdays and Sundays engaged in hobbies which did not include her. During periods of stress he often came home late and frequently was intoxicated. She refused to be a doormat, but would constantly present herself in humility, love and meekness. He would get furious when she talked of her faith that led her to relate as she did. Frequently she suffered a great deal because of her decision to live what she believed God wanted from her. At times he would threaten to leave, and on occasion he would move out. She would suffer the loss only to have him call a few days later, wanting to return. She was torn because, emotionally, she felt it best to terminate the relationship; whereas, spiritually, she felt that as long as he wanted to stay she would support him while he struggled with his emotions. She suffered because she did what she felt God wanted her to do.

In summary, the part of Matthew 5 we call the Beatitudes is contradicting the world. It tells us that spiritual changes will be reflected in the way we relate to God and to others. It tells us that we have been sold a false bill of goods on the kinds of attitudes and behavior that produce happiness. The act of becoming humble can produce more than all the acquisition, competition and ruling attitudes that are encouraged as the way to suc-

cess and happiness. Applying these spiritual principles to our everyday life with our families can
mean the difference between happiness and
endurance. Most people want rich and fulfilled
lives and they do those things that they believe will
produce them. So what are people in America
today doing to gain a sense of happiness? Statis-
tics tell us that the world's standards of success
are creating more misery, not more happiness.
Like lemmings running to the sea and finding no
joy in the process, we are told to run faster with
more intensity; then we will have happiness.

This issue of how to live with God and others
cuts across time. Man's pursuit of happiness has
never allowed him to arrive at his destination, yet
he goes on trying. Living Matthew 5 means letting
go of doing it yourself. That seems to be the bot-
tom line that makes it so very difficult. Can you
give up your life to gain life?

The Beatitudes also say that even those people
we don't consider worthy can be blessed and
happy also. Jesus listed those who were seen as
nothing in their society—those who were, and still
are, looked upon with disdain. How does this
apply to our families? Can you realize the worth
and value God places on people? Those who are fat
can be blessed; those who are bald can be blessed;
those homely kids who have dirty faces and runny
noses and freckles are also included. Then there
are those who are constant complainers; those
who get the checkbook out of balance; those who
are lazy; those who never cooperate; those who
snore; those who are klutzes; those who are out of
style—they can be blessed also. Kids who store
dirty socks under their beds, spill food on the living room carpet, let the dog chew up their clothes,

argue back and are disobedient, embarrass you in front of your friends, leave their jackets at school, break the windows with their baseball and who never listen—they too can be blessed. What Christ is saying is that we divide people into groups—the ins and the outs. We then smugly believe that the ins are blessed of God and the outs are not. We say that we can no longer love our spouse because we have lost respect for him. He is now an out. We can no longer love our kids because they smoke pot and are now outs.

Christ says that all those people we have neatly defined as un-blessable—some of them *are* blessed.

If we love them, see them as valuable people when others judge them unworthy, then we will stand out like a city on a hill.

Questions for Discussion

1. Which of the eight Beatitudes are more difficult for you to apply in your relationships? Which are the easiest?

2. How does "being" as a life-style differ from "accumulating, possessing, and controlling" as a life-style?

3. Can a person pursue happiness and find it? How?

4. Why do we divide people into "in groups" and "out groups" (those we like being the "in group" and those we treat as nonpersons or ignore being the "out group")? Who is in your "out group"? Your "in group"?

5. The Pharisees felt superior to the downtrodden of society and deemed them unblessable. Who is unblessable in your eyes? With what kind of

people do you not relate well?

Notes
1. John MacArthur, Jr., *Kingdom Living Here and Now* (Chicago: Moody Press, 1980).
2. William Jordan as quoted by John G. Quesnell in *Marriage: A Discovery Together* (Notre Dame: Fides/Claretian, 1974).
3. David Augsburger, *Caring Enough to Confront*, rev. ed. (Scottsdale, PA: Herald Press, 1980).

Matthew 5:13-20

You are the salt of the earth; but if the salt loses its flavor, how shall it be seasoned? It is then good for nothing but to be thrown out and trampled underfoot by men. You are the light of the world. A city that is set on a hill cannot be hidden. Nor do they light a lamp and put it under a basket, but on a lampstand, and it gives light to all who are in the house. Let your light so shine before men, that they may see your good works and glorify your Father who is in heaven. Do not think that I have come to destroy the Law or the Prophets. I have not come to destroy but to fulfill. For assuredly, I say to you, till heaven and earth pass away, one jot or one tittle will by no means pass from the law till all is fulfilled. Whoever therefore breaks one of the least of these commandments, and teaches men so, he will be called least in the kingdom of heaven; but whoever does and teaches them will be called great in the kingdom of heaven. For I say to you, that unless your righteousness exceeds the righteousness of the scribes and Pharisees, you will by no means enter the kingdom of heaven.

2

To Be Yourself

Matthew 5:13-20

Following the Beatitudes, Christ makes several interesting follow-up comments that say a great deal about spiritual principles reflected in our relationships. He says that if you are relating in a way that depicts the Kingdom, you will be like salt, a city on a hill, or a light. The concern is that the salt would lose its saltiness and then be worthless. The loss of flavor comes when it becomes just like its surroundings. What happens in a family when people do not show mercy, are not peacemakers, are not humble? They are not interacting in ways that demonstrate Christ's teachings on how to relate to others, and they have lost their effectiveness to preserve the Kingdom Life. They do not stand out from those around them.

When I listen to Christ's teaching, I think He is saying, "Stay in there and be what you should be regardless of what is around you." Husbands and wives often miss this point when they respond to each other based only on the way they are treated.

We are not to become like our surroundings. Yet I think the principle goes much deeper than just saying, "If your wife lets you have it with a barrage of anger, don't respond with anger in return—remain salt and light." The deeper principle seems to be that God has created you as a person whom He knew even before you were born. *He wants you to become the person you were created to be.* If you respond to the world around you by becoming like the world, not only have you lost your very personhood, but a part of His creation is being smothered.

Very often I hear a wife saying, "Sure I'm a nag, but you would be too if you were married to my husband." The implication is that "he makes me what I am by his behavior." She has lost her saltiness. She is no longer her own person but is seen only as a reflection of her husband. She has relinquished her personhood to another. Part of God's creation is lost.

You are to be initiators of God's love, asserting your personhood regardless of the environment. If you continue to be an initiator you will stand out from your environment like Pikes Peak—or at least a city that's highly visible or a bright light on a lampstand. Of course, there is a purpose for this: people will see your good works—that you are superwoman to be able to live with such a beast and still be nice. They will think highly of you, right? Wrong! The purpose is that people will see your good works and *praise your Father in heaven* (see Matt. 5:16). They know that your good works reflect the presence of a Being higher than what they observe in mankind. They know that you, being human, couldn't possibly do that on your own.

In His second teaching, Christ, before leading into some specific principles on how to relate to others, *discredits the righteousness of the Pharisees*. He tells His listeners that unless their righteousness is greater than that of the Pharisees they will never enter the Kingdom of heaven. Can you imagine how shocking that must have been to the ordinary people, let alone the Pharisees? The Pharisees were the religious leaders. They went to church often, tithed, prayed publicly, had at least a working knowledge of the Scripture, and followed the law. They had it all together. But how were they at showing mercy, mourning, desiring to do what Christ told them? How often were they peacemakers?

Christ continues with more directives on relating to other people that again discredit the Pharisees. He says that they could follow the law, but when they lorded it over others, made others into non-persons, returned evil for evil—they were not living in the kingdom. The Pharisees had arrived—they knew the answers. They had the status, they had the power to look down on others and judge them.

Does this ever happen in families? Does a wife ever do all the right things, but lord it over her husband who is weaker? Does a mother ever retaliate with her teenager or get jealous of her daughter who has a flock of boys pursuing her and showering her with attention? Does a husband ever treat his wife like a non-person? Are there ever times when, as head of the house, a husband becomes more repressive than loving?

He went to church faithfully, he studied the Bible by the hour, he knew the Scriptures well and could quote a verse for every situation. He wanted to serve God. He gave of his finances. Yet within his family there were problems. He had little time for his wife and even with encouragement would seldom talk to her. They virtually never did anything together. The kids were nearly grown so they spent most of their time away from home. When he tried to talk with them he mostly contrasted his righteousness to their unrighteousness. They could do nothing right. Eventually they learned to avoid him because of his sharp comments. He carried a great deal of anger and frustration which other people sensed, so they found him unpleasant to be around. He and his wife stayed together but were married only on paper. In terms of being married by virtue of a close relationship that builds into a sense of unity, they were not married. The family did not feel the love of God balanced against the law of God.

Starting in verse 21, Christ continues telling us how to treat and relate to other people. Certainly this has great application to everyday life within our families. Beginning in verse 21 through the end of chapter 7, there seems to me to be 14 principles on how to treat others. These principles are evidence of living in the Kingdom of God—they are not rules to live by. Since they are truth, they work to produce a viable and freed-up family life. They cause people to grow. The following chapters will deal with these 14 principles.

Questions for Discussion

1. In what ways do we become like our surroundings? How can we be more "salty"?

2. Who are the people who influence our behavior the most? How can we assert our personhood regardless of our environment?

3. How can we become the people we were created to be?

4. In what ways are we like the Pharisees? What can we do to change?

5. Can you think of any situation in which someone responded to you being like a city on a hill?

Matthew 5:21-24

You have heard that it was said to those of old, "You shall not murder," and whoever murders will be in danger of the judgment. But I say to you that whoever is angry with his brother without a cause will be in danger of the judgment. And whoever says to his brother, "Racca!" will be in danger of the council. But whoever says, "You fool!" will be in danger of hell fire. Therefore if you bring your gift to the altar, and there remember that your brother has something against you, leave your gift there before the altar, and go your way. First be reconciled to your brother, and then come and offer your gift.

3

Dealing with Your Anger

Matthew 5:21-24

Jesus begins to point out to the people the importance of how to treat others, and particularly how to deal with their anger in relationships (Matt. 5:21,22). He tells them about literally destroying others physically and compares that to the judgment they receive if they destroy others by treating them with contempt.

My understanding of the historical context of this passage is that, in those days, if a person broke the law he could be brought before the judge; if it were a more serious crime he could be brought before a council of 70 men and, if convicted, he could be killed and his body burned at the edge of town in a place called Gehenna.

Here we see the progressive results of mistreating others. With anger, you can be brought before the judge, but if you call someone a fool, you are really at risk. What does it mean to call a person a fool? It is not simply a matter of saying the words, "You fool"; it is when you treat someone as if he is a "fool" or, in other words, as a person of no worth. When your anger is used in such a way as to destroy the worth of a person who in fact has infinite worth in God's eyes, then this may be just as detrimental to your relationship with God as if you had killed the person physically.

By treating others as if they have no worth, you destroy their very personhood. In the view of God, people are much more than physical beings. In fact, we are taught that we should not fear those who can destroy merely the physical aspect of our natures. In this passage Jesus says that we should be aware not only of the fact that we can destroy physically, but also that we can destroy by treating people as non-persons or as persons of no worth. Does this ever happen in the righteous, upright, church-attending family that can never see themselves murdering anyone?

She and he were both active members of their church. He was the head of the family and would get very angry if his wife ever threatened or questioned his authority. Therefore, he made all the decisions in the family, and she acquiesced to them. There were times when she had a different opinion but she seldom expressed it. He could always come up with valid reasons to contradict her. She learned to keep her opinions to herself and also to devalue them since he was always right.

He had few questions for her because he had all the answers. Often he would tell her how to clean the house, how to shop, how to prepare the food. Frequently he was in the kitchen telling her the how and wherefores. Over the years she became a non-person—in his eyes, and later in her own eyes, she became a person of no worth. He knew it all along since his father, in his own anger toward women, had treated his mother in the same way. Now the sins of one generation were being passed to the next.

You could never convince him that he had done anything that led to the destruction of another. He was convinced that he was only doing his job as the husband. He never questioned the way his father had treated his mother nor the results in her, so why would he review what he was doing? Likewise, he never wondered about what was happening in his relationship, because he knew all the answers. When you have the answers you can't grow, because there are no further questions to ask yourself. He had become a closed person. He noticed his wife becoming less expressive and more dependent on him for answers, but he assumed this was because she did not have answers to life's questions. He even liked her dependence; it made him feel better about himself as he rapidly and efficiently dispersed many solutions.

In addition to ongoing, seething anger is the more explosive kind of anger. The wife who is deeply hurt when her husband does not fulfill her expectation that he be like her father and dote on her when she has a difficult day, tells him what she thinks. He is an insensitive person who has nothing to offer anybody. He has never been a good husband and never will be and she should have married someone who had more character. She has lost all respect for him and thinks he is a nothing of a man. Suddenly, in her anger, her request and need for more attention have turned into a character assault on her husband. His personhood has been laid to waste. Christ is saying, "The law says don't murder. I say, in your anger don't treat people as if they are worthless" (see Matt. 5:21,22).

Then there are the kids. Being good parents, neither of you ever disciplines out of anger, right? There are times every parent disciplines out of anger, particularly when parents see characteristics in their children that are the character traits they dislike most in themselves. Then there are also those parents who need their children to succeed because they are trying to live their lives out through the children. Therefore, the parents become very distressed at the children's misbehavior. How does a parent then discipline in a way that does not destroy the value and worth of the child? The principle still applies—do not treat children as worthless in the way you deal with your anger toward them. This is not meant to be a book about discipline of children; therefore it would not be reasonable to discuss methodology at this time. Whatever the method you use, it needs to be administered in such a way that the child's personhood is not disrupted. This means that the focus must be on the deed and on changing behavior, not on the child's character.

Likewise there are children who receive the brunt of the family's frustration and anger in an ongoing system that keeps them in this role. The mother or father cannot express anger directly toward the other and, therefore, takes it out on one of the children. The child becomes the family scapegoat. He is treated as a worthless person.

He was 13 and raised in a structured Christian family that had many rules. Yet, his father, who was under his own emotional stress, would constantly lash out at him in anger. The boy's feelings and needs in the home were not really dealt with and nobody seemed particularly interested in dealing with them. His sister, following the prevailing attitude taught by her mother, would assert herself and ignore her brother's needs because ladies' needs should be considered first. The mother told him openly that she considered him the worst of children, although he was not considered a behavior problem by others. He became a worthless person—beaten down by his family. He was treated as if he were a fool.

A more difficult and insidious anger is that expressed by withdrawal. The parent is never openly angry at the child; he or she is just never around. Jean was 14 when she came to see me. Her parents were separated. It had been months since her father had called or seen her. Her mother was busy with her own life and was working, so she had no time for her. Coming home from school each evening, Jean did her homework, prepared herself a meal and spent the evening alone. Her parents were not openly angry with her but the message was clear—we do not value you. She felt worthless. In their anger and insensitivity they simply withdrew from caring about her.

To treat others in the way Christ taught involves respect and worth. If we can recognize that the other person is created in the image of God and can understand His love for him, it only follows that he should not have his value assaulted.

Whenever anger exists between two people, the relationship is broken. We need to be aware of the brokenness of relationships. We need to establish a reuniting of the people involved.

Many times when anger flares up in a family it is repressed or denied or ignored. A husband will be angry at his wife for what he perceives as an offense, but he will say to himself, "I don't want the hassle—I'll just let it slide." Or the wife will be angry at her husband and feel she can never get through to him, so why bother. The principle being taught here is to not allow anger to continue between you and another person; rather, deal with the anger. Christ knew what worked and what didn't work in relationships. That is why He encouraged people to be reconciled. When anger exists, a wall is created and people are cut off from each other; therefore, they can neither give nor receive love from each other. In addition, they, as individuals, are left to deal with their own personal isolation and frustration.

Not dealing with anger has a cumulative effect. An angry person can very well develop into a bitter or depressed person. At this stage the anger becomes even *more* difficult to handle. Christ's encouragement reflects Proverbs 17:14. When anger is beginning, it needs to be dealt with then, just like fixing the first leak in a dam before the water breaks out.

They were married for about 10 years; both were now in their mid-thirties. They had two children whom they loved dearly. They had never had a lot of conflict—she had always been a cooperative wife. One day she finally told him that for several years she had not felt anything for him. She was now indifferent. She described feeling no love at all. Over the years she had been angry many times; this anger had never been resolved. Now her love was frozen by the accumulation of anger that had actually started back in childhood when she was the model compliant daughter on the outside— angry inside. Dr. Sam Keen describes it this way: "You wake up one morning. It is February in your soul. The tide is out and nothing is visible except mud flats. There isn't much pain, just emptiness. The excitement of living has ebbed away, leaving only a littered line of memories along the shore to mark the receding tide of passion."[1]

Anger is often avoided because family members feel uncomfortable with it. Perhaps it reminds them of parents being angry at them when they were children. It stirs fear. I find anger often described as a negative emotion. Certainly, considering the way it is expressed at times, it can be viewed as such; but I am not sure it has to be defined this way. Whenever your spouse or child is angry at you or you at them, it is important to realize that anger is not the opposite of love. The opposite of love is indifference. The people you care about the most, and who are emotionally involved with you the most, are those with whom you will feel the greatest intensity of emotion. Therefore, realize that the other person's anger, in that sense, is also saying, "I am involved with you." It shows they care.

Anger also carries with it a demand for some change. At the root of the other person's anger (or your own anger) is some form of pain or threat of pain. Most of the time this comes from a feeling of rejection or disappointment when an expectation was not fulfilled. It then follows that people most sensitive to feeling rejected (because of childhood experiences), and those who set up many expectations for others, are the ones who are most easily angered. When anger comes up, it is important to deal with the pain and hurt in the relationship and not simply get caught up in the anger. When you read about God's anger in the Old Testament, look at the context and see His concern about Israel rejecting His love for them.

Although I do not recall the author, my favorite definition of anger is "wounded love." When one understands this dynamic, he is better able to deal with his own as well as other family members' anger. It does not seem to be the monster we make it out to be. When we see that, then the energy from the anger can be used to bring reconciliation into the relationship. Christ's goal in Matthew 5:23,24 seems to be to encourage people to deal with their anger, not ignore it.

Questions for Discussion

1. In what ways do we imply that others are "fools"?

2. What are some nonverbal ways of communicating the following attitudes to people?
   a. anger
   b. you good-for-nothing
   c. you worthless fool

3. If anger is an emotion that we are supposed to feel, what are its distinctive expressions? What are its constructive expressions?

4. How is anger most often handled by various members of your family? Discuss these three ways of dealing with anger:
   a. repression
   b. expression
   c. confession

5. What is the root of stubbornness that causes people to refuse reconciliation?

Note

1. Sam Keen, "Chasing the Blahs Away: Boredom and How to Beat It." *Psychology Today*, (May, 1977), pp. 78-80.

Matthew 5:25,26

Agree with your adversary quickly, while you are on the way with him, lest your adversary deliver you to the judge, the judge hand you over to the officer, and you are thrown into prison. Assuredly, I say to you, you will by no means get out of there till you have paid the last penny.

4

Be Willing to Be Reconciled
Matthew 5:25,26

There is a desire on God's part to see men reconciled with each other rather than involved in disputes. Jesus, in Matthew 5:25,26, is emphasizing that you should not just be defensive but should seek reconciliation even when someone is really upset at you and about to make you pay through the nose. When being threatened with legal action you're better off reaching an agreement out of court. I do not believe Christ is saying just reach an agreement so it will be easier on you. He is saying that if you are unwilling to reach an agreement, it may be even more difficult for you and you can potentially suffer even more.

There are times in families when people get stubborn. They are threatened in some way and deal with that threat by refusing to reconcile. They use their anxiety and anger to block restoration of the relationship.

They were 23 and 24. Betsy was really angry at

Paul because he wanted to be at his friend's house working on Todd's car all the time. They had been married only eight months and she was feeling ignored. So on Friday night she decided to be gone when he arrived home at 11:00 P.M. Her plan was to give him a dose of his own medicine. He came home and was worried. When she showed up at 1:00 A.M. he was really upset and that set off the argument that led her to threaten to leave. His response was, "Fine, I can't think of a better idea—get out." Down inside, he did not want her to go and would really miss her if she left. Yet he couldn't tell her that, or so he thought. He was threatened, so he fought back harder than ever. He refused to work toward reconciliation. The results could have been disastrous had she not had the presence of mind, and a desire to reconcile, that brought about a change in her attitude once she calmed down. The principle seems to say, Think of the difficulty that can come when you refuse to reach an agreement that will bring reconciliation to the relationship.

What then do we do with anger if we are not to treat the other as worthless? Jesus goes on to say that when we realize that our brother has something against us, we should go to him and be reconciled. I believe that the Bible does not teach us to not be angry but rather to *deal* with our anger.

I find it interesting that Jesus places such a great emphasis on relationships that—at least timewise—they take priority over worship. The other fascinating point is that, in this case, Jesus is not talking about the person who is angry going to worship. For He says, "If you remember that someone is upset *at you*—go and be reconciled." If a father knows his daughter is angry at him, he should go and discuss the issue with her. Their relationship needs to be reconciled rather than leaving it with wounds to fester.

Why do people avoid dealing with the anger of others? Sometimes I think it is because they misunderstand what the Bible says about anger. Some believe that since they are Christians they should never be angry. There are passages, such as Proverbs 15:1 and 17:14, that seem to teach that Christians will feel anger. In fact, I am told that the Old Testament says that God was angry at the nation Israel 365 times! We are taught to be slow to anger—Proverbs 16:32; to control anger—Proverbs 25:28; to not provoke others to anger—Colossians 3:21; and to put it away—Ephesians 4:31. But I don't find anywhere that it says you'll never feel it. I talked to a Christian man a couple of months ago who told me that he never got angry since he became a Christian. As I watched him put down others, saw his unhappiness, his tightly-drawn and stern face, and heard his forceful, hard voice, I realized he was the angriest person I had ever seen.

Part of dealing with anger involves recognizing what it is and then working through it with the other person. *The first step for dealing with anger is to own your anger.* You cannot deal with anger until you own it and it clearly belongs to you. By pointing the finger at the other person you make the assumption that he is the one who needs change in order for you not to be angry. In so doing, you relinquish the control and responsibility of your life to others. It is your hurt. You own it. The rejection you feel is dependent on your interpretation of the other's behavior. The husband forgets to bring home the bread that his wife asked him to stop and pick up. She is angry. She tells herself, "He never listens to me. He doesn't care about what I have to say—he doesn't care about me." Now comes the rejection and anger. She could just as well have told herself, "He doesn't listen—well, he has had a busy day at work and was preoccupied with his own insecurity about his job. I know he still cares for me. He is just human."

Since your anger is dependent on how you interpret another's behavior or words, you control it. Therefore, it belongs to you.

The second step for dealing with anger is to go and confess the feeling to the other person, owning your own anger. This involves describing what changes you would like from the other person and then searching for his cooperation. It takes two steps—*sharing your feeling* and *seeking a solution*. The idea is not to blame him for your anger nor to accuse him. By following these steps you can direct the energy from the anger toward reconciliation rather than toward destruction of the other's personhood.

The only other options for dealing with anger are (1) to *push it aside* or (2) to *act it out*. The first is to bottle it up inside and control, control, control the expression of it. You know you're angry, but your spouse doesn't. If you really repress it well, it may be hidden even from yourself—although others may see it.

The other option is to, in some way, act it out—slam doors, don't talk, stomp out of the room, hit, yell, etc. Neither of these options works well because they both impact the relationship so strongly in a form that is more difficult to deal with and ultimately is more disruptive. The first option often leads to physical problems like back-aches, headaches or depression, while the second often leads to defensiveness and more anger in return.

In this sermon, Christ recognizes that there will be times when you are angry. He is saying that in working out anger with other people, don't treat them as if they are worthless non-people. Rather He tells us to go to them and be reconciled. His emphasis is on healing and restoration of relationships, not destruction.

Questions for Discussion

1. Why is it so difficult to admit anger? In what ways do you keep from owning your anger?

2. What happens when you refuse to take the first step toward reconciliation? What might happen if you do take that step?

3. What factors in families contribute to people not being reconciled?

4. In what ways are people treated as worthless non-persons when being the recipients of anger?

5. What is the long-term effect on a family that has a pattern of non-reconciliation?

Matthew 5:27-32

You have heard that it was said to those of old, "You shall not commit adultery." But I say to you that whoever looks at a woman to lust for her has already committed adultery with her in his heart. And if your right eye causes you to sin, pluck it out and cast it from you; for it is profitable for you that one of your members perish, and not that your whole body be cast into hell. And if your right hand causes you to sin, cut it off and cast if from you; for it is profitable for you that one of your members perish, and not that your whole body be cast into hell. Furthermore it has been said, "Whoever puts away his wife, let him give her a certificate of divorce." But I say to you that whoever divorces his wife, except for sexual immorality, causes her to commit adultery; and whoever marries a woman who is divorced commits adultery.

5

Thinking About Others

Matthew 5:27-32

In Matthew 5:27-32, using the illustration of adultery, Christ teaches about the importance of the inner person. He tells us that even if we don't actually have an affair, if we look at another woman with fantasies of a sexual relationship, we have committed adultery.

Perhaps this illustration was chosen by Christ because He knew that the men in the crowd could at least somewhat relate to it. He was not saying to them that they should feel guilty about their human sexuality; He was telling them that they needed to be aware of how they *thought* about people. There seems to be a point at which we can, through the use of visual imagery, commit all kinds of wrongful relationships with other people—relationships that God considers sin. It is also a reminder that God does indeed look upon a man's heart and not just at his behavior.

One could speculate that Jesus was also concerned that if a person dwelt on his fantasy life long enough, he might begin to act it out in real life.

There is a broader principle here in that He is emphasizing the inner, spiritual life as opposed to just a physical life. We see here the importance of another way of life, emphasized as a priority over the physical. Christ is not describing His desire to see people mutilate themselves in some fashion in order to be holy. He is saying that, in level of importance, there is another world that takes precedence over the tangible world in which we live. He is saying that the spiritual realm is just as much a part of reality as the physical realm. Just because there are some phenomena that we cannot actually see does not mean that these phenomena are not a part of reality.

So how does the way we treat people in the inner person affect relationships? If we regard others with wrong motives, hatred, or disrepute, God is still very much aware of what is happening. He is likewise concerned about it. He is concerned that the inner person have the proper relationship to others just as He is concerned that the outer person treat others in a way that reflects the mind of God. If there are factors in the tangible world that are disruptive to the inner person, these should be seen as having lesser importance in comparison to the inner world.

Christ is teaching by comparison again when He starts out by saying, "You have heard,. . . but I am saying." He is attempting to refocus our attention to a new concept of viewing the world we live in day to day. This world should include an awareness of how we think about other people. Inside do we use other people for our own pleasure or do we really care about them?

We are taught that "as a man thinketh so is he" (Prov. 23:7). If a person has one set of thoughts internally he will either express these externally or will have to pretend to others that he is something different from what he is on the inside. Either way, external relationships are greatly affected. People are used instead of being accepted, or relationships break down because of the distance created by deception. In some situations the inner life becomes hidden from the person himself because it is too unacceptable. He employs defense mechanisms that still create internal stress as well as emotional distance from others.

This lesson can be a valuable one in relation to your own family. People should be aware of how they think about each other. Here Christ used the illustration of sexuality, but the principle goes well beyond that one area and is much more inclusive. The question has to do with whether people are used or cared about internally. One wonders if Christ could not have made a similar statement to the child who is brooding in her room about all the nifty ways to get back at Mom for disciplining her. What about the wife who has all kinds of fantasies for retaliating toward her husband because he yelled at her and called her a bitch?

We need to become aware of how we are thinking about others, particularly those in our own families.

Questions for Discussion

1. If you think about a person in a harmful way, how does this thought affect your relationship?

2. Why is thinking about adultery just the same in God's eyes as committing adultery?

3. What might be some intangibles that are real but not a part of the physical world we live in?

4. How do family members sometimes abuse others and themselves by their thought life?

Matthew 5:38,39

You have heard that it has been said, "An eye for an eye and a tooth for a tooth." But I tell you not to resist an evil person. But whoever slaps you on your right cheek, turn the other to him also.

6

No Evil Returned
Matthew 5:38,39

In essence, Christ is saying, "I know that you have learned it one way, but I am teaching you a new way of relating. When your wife criticizes you, don't condemn her back. When your son ignores what you have asked of him, deal with it, but treat him personally with respect. When your husband belittles you in front of others, talk kindly with him about not doing it again. Do not retaliate." (See Matt. 5:38,39.)

In Exodus 21, God gave the laws necessary for the Jewish nation to function. We must keep in mind that at that time there was no separation of church and state. The church was also the government. There they were taught an eye for an eye and a tooth for a tooth, a hand for a hand, a foot for a foot, a burning for a burning, a wound for a wound, a stripe for a stripe and even a life for a life. We read the same concept in Leviticus 24 and Deuteronomy 19. Matthew 5, then, contrasts living in the Kingdom with living under the Law.

The message seems to be that, even though a person has done something evil, we are not to respond in the same manner. The old concept was: you caused me to suffer, therefore you shall receive punishment in return. The new concept is one of grace, mercy and forgiveness which, in turn, reflects Christ. Sometimes husbands and wives go even one step beyond, returning punishment by finding a reason to *justify* the punishment. "She constantly nags so I'll really hurt her feelings. That way she will learn her lesson. She will be a better person. It will shape her up and she will change." Now he has a wonderful excuse to return evil. After all, how can you fault a husband for causing his wife to improve? The surface rationale is that it's for her own good.

The problem from a practical point of view is that you don't get people to change by beating on them in some fashion. How often have you ever changed your spouse by using some form of punishment? People do not change for the better by being the recipient of some form of evil.

Bob had a habit of leaving his shoes and the newspaper all over the living room. Anna had asked him innumerable times simply to pick them up when finished, or on his way to bed. Inside he was hoping for a wife who would be like a mother and look after him. He simply blocked out her request. On this night she finally had it. The frustration peaked. When she discovered his shoes she decided once and for all to fix him for all the distress she felt he was dishing out to her. She stomped into the bedroom, woke him up by yelling at him while throwing his shoes and papers all over. She concluded her tantrum by stomping out and sleeping on the couch. For a few days he picked up his shoes and paper. She felt she had finally reached him. Then a few weeks later she realized he was back into the old routine. In fact, on nights he was feeling rebellious, it was even worse.

Not returning evil for evil is not teaching passivity in the sense of weakness. You are not taught to become a doormat on which people wipe their emotional feet. If a spouse or child hands you some evil, it does not mean that you ignore it or refuse to deal with it. The point here is that you don't deal with it in a sense of punishment without regard for the well-being of the other person. There is a vast difference between the husband who responds to his wife's nagging by saying, "Nag, nag, nag. That's all you ever do because you're too stupid to offer anything of intelligence," and the husband who says, "I feel like you're often pressuring me into doing things. I really think we need to talk about how we handle jobs that you want me to do but which I don't complete." Guess which form of relating builds relationships and which destroys people? Which way reflects the way God relates to us? The key point is not to avoid the issue. The critical part is how you treat the other person when you feel you have not been treated well.

There are several reasons that make this principle difficult to apply in families. *The first reason has to do with the issue of rights.* People believe they have rights. They have a right to be treated fairly 100 percent of the time. They have a right to not ever have anybody mistreat them. They have a right to expect the rest of the family to always be nice to them. Because they view themselves as having all these inalienable rights, they then demand that their rights be fulfilled. What rights does a person have in a family beyond that of loving others? There is such a difference between the view that "I have rights that absolutely must be fulfilled" and thinking, "I hope I am treated fairly most of the time. I desire that people are not hostile toward me, but I know that some of the time they will be. If people are angry or unfair, I am not going to allow that to destroy my happiness."

If a person tells himself that he has to have all of his rights fulfilled in order to be happy, the relationship is immediately under great pressure. The chances of not returning evil for evil become slim at best. Expectations make a great difference in the amount of pressure that comes from dealing with rights. It has been said that marital happiness is the difference between what you expect and what you get. When a person's focus is on getting his rights, it is very easy to accumulate a lot of "I owe you's." "He ignored my needs to talk this evening so I'll ignore his needs for support with his pressure from his job."

The second reason that becomes a hurdle in not returning evil for evil is that of not understanding anger. It is often when one spouse is angry at the other that evil is passed back and forth like a hot potato. I have discussed the dynamics of anger in the previous chapter. When your spouse or child is really angry, it remains important to not get caught on this hook, but rather to get at the root issue of their experienced pain. It is much easier to not return evil when you are not overwhelmed by the other's anger. If you feel threatened and return even more, the issues are soon lost in the smoke of the battle.

Another concept that makes it difficult to not return evil for evil is that of "getting even." Children go through a phase of development during their elementary school years when they compare themselves to others and want everything to be the same or to be even. If you give each a glass of Coke, they will measure down to the millimeter to see who got the most. It is from this need to see things equal that you get the returning equal evil. If somebody does you wrong, your main goal in life is to get even. This same childhood concept carries into adulthood, particularly for some adults who felt that they were bullied or mistreated by an older brother or sister. They have developed a low threshold for being mistreated. Their immediate response is to equalize things by getting even. They then carry their past with them into their own families where it surfaces again and again. Yet nobody ever said that it is your job to even out interactions between people. It does not automatically follow that things have to be evened out or that every negative action deserves a negative reaction. Why should things in life be equal? The process of constant comparison to others and attempts to equalize everything leads one into conflict and stress rather than into freedom.

Christ goes on, in Matthew 20, to give the parable of the vineyard owner who paid those who worked one hour the same as those who worked all day. The workers were not treated very evenly, which really upset those who worked all day. The Lord does not think things have to be even-steven between people. There really is no reason that you have to get back at someone to even out the mistreatment. The other person doesn't deserve to be mistreated in return.

They were a young couple who had grown up through difficult experiences. He was very assertive and somewhat hostile, while she was likewise self-assured and assertive. There were times when their wills clashed since both were opinionated as to what they liked and didn't like. She was a graduate student and planning a career. He discovered she had been unfaithful to him, which is always a very painful experience. His way of dealing with it, however, was not to try to work out the relationship, but rather to retaliate. He attacked her at the most important point of her life, which was her career. He went to professors, deans, etc., and made every attempt to have her thrown out of graduate school so he could destroy the most valued thing in her life. He was attempting to gain vengeance for his own hurt. He may have gained some sense of vengeance but was never successful in his attempts to have her thrown out of graduate school. They struggled with their relationship which she eventually terminated.

With kids it is the same principle, but the situations are different. Suppose you ask the kids not to play in the house with their friends when you're not home. They ignore you, bring in their friends, begin roughhousing and tear the upholstery on the good sofa. If you are immediately angry and want them to suffer because they have caused you to suffer, then you are sliding into returning evil. You need to be concerned about discipline but also to consider the well-being of the person. This is the difference between punishment and discipline.

On some occasions, people will tell me, "I can't help it. When he comes into the house, I see his anger. And when he starts in on me, I just strike back. It is impossible for me not to do so. It's not something I plan—it's just a reaction." It may well be true that, as an adult, there are situations left over from childhood that cause you to well up with emotion instantly. This does not mean that you have to turn control of yourself over to your feelings. Making the assumption that you have to do whatever you feel has grave consequences. By labeling and dismissing an emotion as a "reaction," somehow a person is supposed to be relieved of the responsibility for his behavior. If the feelings are intense, then it is useful to be aware of them.

Likewise it is useful to obtain the assistance of another person to think back into childhood to discover if the roots of this reaction really have their beginning with another relationship. How did you feel about the anger of a parent or sibling? Was there a parent who was overly angry at you? If so, how does that impact the way you feel about others being angry at you now? Dealing with anger or mistreatment may stir lots of old feelings, but you still do not have to return evil for evil. You are never tempted above what you are able to bear; so in each situation the choice of response is still a viable option.

In this passage, Christ does not seem to distinguish between levels of evil received. He does not say, "If someone does something that is a little evil to you, let it slide; but if what he does is really rotten, then let him have it." He simply says, "Don't return it." At times a spouse will hurt you deeply by lashing out in a way he/she knows you are particularly vulnerable. This is much more serious than a mild dig, because it cuts you right to the quick. The depth of your hurt makes this principle more difficult to apply, but perhaps it also makes it more important to apply.

Barry came home from work to find that Laura, his teenage daughter from his first marriage, was in tears. She had been arguing with Connie, her stepmother. He dreaded being in the middle again and wished he could avoid the whole confrontation. Connie was really angry when he sided with Laura. Barry didn't realize how protective he had been with her. Laura knew that no matter what, her dad would always come to her rescue. Connie felt like an outsider trying to raise someone else's daughter. She was really frustrated by her husband's permissiveness. Laura was told by her father that she would not need to be grounded for not turning in her report at school, but he did ask that she do her work. Connie was furious that he undercut her authority. Her voice was sharp, tense and pressured as she told Barry exactly what she thought of him and how he was ruining Laura's life. Laura had left the room with a sense of satisfaction, so Barry felt free to tell Connie what a harsh, overly critical and jealous wife she had become. The next day, Connie was more determined than ever to not let Laura get away with one more thing. She found evidence of pot in her room while looking through the dresser drawers. Now she had her for sure and planned to confront Barry the instant he walked in the door. She couldn't wait until he got home.

On and on the family went, month after month. Attack—counterattack—accusation—denial—force—resistance. Their lives were a continual running battle that nobody enjoyed. Yet they continued their miserable existence blow for blow, flailing their way through life.

Do not return evil for evil. If slapped, turn the other cheek.

Questions for Discussion

1. Why do you think Christ continued to contrast the people's ideas ("the law," or "you have read") with His teachings ("but I say")?

2. What makes returning evil for evil so easy to do?

3. Is there ever a time that a person is justified in returning evil?

4. Do people in the family have a right to be treated in a certain way? From where do "rights" originate?

5. What might be some examples of not returning evil for evil that could apply in your family?

Matthew 5:40

And if anyone wants to sue you and take away your tunic, let him have your cloak also.

7

Taken Advantage Of
Matthew 5:40

The next principle is that of how to handle a person who takes something away from you that belongs to you. (See Matthew 5:40.)

When I read these principles that Christ is teaching the people as a life-style, I keep wondering, "How can He ask such things of people—is He serious?" He is serious. I can understand how these principles would revolutionize family life when applied. They sound idealistic. But are they?

I shall never forget seeing this principle of giving more expressed on television. The program was one where they were interviewing couples who were celebrating their fiftieth wedding anniversary. The interviewer asked the couples to share their secret of success for being married 50 years. He came to one spry little old lady whose eyes sparkled like that of a teenager. She was obviously a happy person. She said her advice was this: "Right at the start of the marriage, demand that it be a

50-50 relationship when it comes to giving and taking. Then you give 75 percent, but don't ever tell him you're doing it."

Part of understanding this principle is the awareness of who owns what. When people take advantage of you, what are you really losing? If you conceive of that which you have as yours, you become possessive and preservation-oriented. But suppose you begin to realize that everything you have does not belong to you? Perhaps your car, your ability to think, your attractive appearance, your ability to love, and even your ability to draw your next breath are all things granted to you from God. Suppose every good gift and every perfect gift is from the Father and comes down from above? Then you are a steward, rather than an owner. It then makes more sense that if someone takes something of yours, it may not be the end of the world.

"But I am not going to let people take advantage of me. I must stand up for myself." I do not see this passage as a request for Christians to be martyrs. The life-style of most people is one of taking care of the things which they have. This passage should lead people to freedom, not to fear. We do not need fear. Those who are martyrs must legalistically allow everyone who comes along to take advantage of them. Christ is not saying that this is some new legalistic way to deal with others, for then we have no choice and it is just another rule. He does tell us a radically new way of handling an issue when someone does take advantage on occasion. He calls our attention to the one Who is ultimately in control of the universe.

There are also points of struggle within each person that make us vulnerable. We can be taken advantage of in these areas. Suppose she is not a strong person. Her fear of rejection and insecurity lead her to agree with others rather than take a stand for what she believes. Her husband and kids know if they push long enough and hard enough, she will give in to them. They have won, she has lost. If she resists, they simply imply they won't talk to her, which floods her with fears of rejection and she knuckles under. They know the right buttons to push. Does she have the opportunity to apply this principle? Not until she gains the strength to be able to say no to them and have a true choice. You cannot give a coat to the one taking your shirt until you have a coat that you can choose to give. The wife and mother so wrapped in her insecurity does not have the chance to give in this way, for she is not in a position to choose to do so.

I wonder how far beyond tangible items Christ meant this to apply. I do not think He wants people to allow others to take advantage of them to the point of losing their personhood. I cannot envision Him encouraging a wife to give up her identity because her husband takes advantage of his role and tries to remake her into a copy of himself. Nor do I think of children giving up their worthiness because parents treat them as if they had no worth. I am advised, however, by a friend who went through a life experience of this nature, that God does call people to give up more for a season when they are in some way being taken advantage of. In his case it climaxed in a time of great personal growth for him, his wife and their family. I do not think, however, that God always ends on such a rosy note. You may give up your coat also and He may never replace it with a better one. The issue is growth—spiritual maturity—not replacement.

In a family when a shirt is taken, there is a strong tendency to fight back rather than give more. The wife has asked the husband to help clean the house during a time when he has a lot of pressure at work. She has been doing little housework herself, so her request is not fair. Then comes Saturday, and in his head he plans a day of relaxation. Saturday morning she lets him know that she wants him to scrub the kitchen walls. If you were this husband, what would be your first response?

Often people make assessments as to whether the other person deserves their assistance or not. By using this measurement of deserving, you can usually come up with good reasons to do or not to do almost anything. People are very gifted at finding excellent reasons to do whatever they decide they want to do. The process usually involves deciding what you want to do and then coming up with the reasons.

There is a valid cause for assessment of reason, but that type of assessment is probably used infrequently. You do need to assess what impact your actions will have on the other person. For example, is it really building or edifying for the spouse if you help clean the walls? Could it in some way be destructive? This principle would dictate that you do that which is best for the spouse. Perhaps your wife has grown up in a family that overprotected her to the point that she is a rather helpless, dependent person. In that situation, you may decide to *help her* scrub the walls rather than doing them yourself. Your goal is very clear. You encourage, assist and build her up so as to help her achieve a greater sense of self-sufficiency and confidence. For you to do the task alone would only reinforce her dependency.

The next time you feel taken advantage of by your kids or spouse, consider giving your coat also. In doing this you can see why you would be like a saltshaker or a light shining brightly. People cannot help but notice you and pause to wonder at what you are doing.

Questions for Discussion

1. Where in the Bible did you see an example of a person giving even more after someone had taken advantage of him?

2. How do we come to the conclusion that we own tangible property instead of being stewards?

3. Have you ever given more to someone who was taking advantage of you? What was the result?

4. What might be some everyday examples of giving more when being taken advantage of that would apply in our homes?

5. What does possessing something and refusing to let go of it do to our spiritual and emotional growth?

Matthew 5:41

And whoever shall compel you to go one mile, go with him two.

8

Dealing with Force

Matthew 5:41

The next principle, Matthew 5:41, is an interesting one because it again deals with issues that have been faced primarily in childhood. Consequently, it brings to the surface all those old feelings from childhood. How do you handle a situation where somebody forces you to do something you do not want to do? Verse 41 says that you should not only do what they want, but even do more! The people in that day and age understood the principle in context of the Roman soldiers who sometimes imposed upon the local folks. They would make them carry their heavy armor for them. So Jesus says, "Look, if some Roman soldier comes along and makes you carry his armor for a mile, you willingly carry it two miles." I am certain the Roman soldier's attitude was one of disregard for the people and a lack of concern for their plans at the time of forceful imposition. What could be more difficult? They didn't want the Romans there in the first place. They didn't like being forced out of their routine. But Christ says to do even more.

Most people want to be the sender of coercion, not the receiver. Husbands and wives find all kinds of wonderful ways to force the other or their kids into doing what they want. For some, force is verbal skills. They can outthink and outtalk the other. Others use threats both blatant (I'll leave) and subtle (not responding well), withholding themselves from the relationship if the other doesn't shape up. Others use physical violence. Sometimes Christians even get good at quoting Bible verses in an effort to force the spouse or kids into some set of behaviors. Other individuals are able to bring great pressure to bear on their spouses or kids by the use of weakness or guilt. These methods are much more powerful than a direct confrontation. Families expend a great deal of time and energy pressuring other family members into thinking a certain way, doing or not doing certain behaviors. Therefore, every family member deals every day with the issue of force even though it may not be conspicuous.

There is a sense in which we can be in control of ourselves and still decide to be giving when other people force us. Perhaps when the pressure starts coming you may decide to respond to your spouse rather than to dig in your heels and prove to him/her that he/she can't make you do anything. The struggle for control of self, which starts in childhood when junior says no to his parents' request to pick up his toys, does not have to be continued in adult family life. Certainly the more freedom and less pressure family members place on one another, the less force there will be to deal with. This makes for a much improved atmosphere in which to live.

Much of the resistance to being forced has to do with proving to the spouse that he can't make the other one do anything. Proving to another person that you are the more powerful is real one-upmanship. Is this then not the process of elevating one's self over the spouse? You are back to being just like the Pharisees, whom we often talk about as the bad example. Their problem was that they were always busy proving that they were better than others. They liked especially to be more righteous. That was the ultimate upmanship. Christ said that the first would be last and the last first, so you should put others ahead of yourself. The only problem with the Pharisees is that they are merely extensions of what we see in all of us. Perhaps an unconscious recognition that there are a lot of similarities may well prompt the uncomfortableness and consequent negativism toward the Pharisees.

The more couples are able to let go and respond to the needs of each other, even when expressed with force, the more freedom the relationship has in it. The more force is met with counterforce, the more tense the relationship. Christ calls us in life to be willing to let go of family, possessions, status. Why would we think it unusual that He also call upon us to let go of self-power in order to follow Him? Certainly He let go of His own power to come to earth in the first place. It seems that much of what He taught had to do with letting go of the self-power that we use to provide our own sense of self-security. Perhaps He also wants us to trust Him to take care of relationships with others. Perhaps He wants us to trust Him to take care of them and not rely on our own ability to out-power others.

You can apply this Matthew principle with children, while keeping in mind their maturity level and their development of a concept of authority. Certainly this does not mean that when you want five-year-old Susie to go to bed at 8:00 and she tries to force you to let her stay up until 9:00, that you should ultimately let her stay up until 10:00. Kids need to have limits placed on them by adults who have the maturity to look out for their best interests. However, there are times when children force parents in ways to which parents can respond. You have had a busy day getting everyone off in the morning, trying to catch up on the laundry, and getting through a hectic dinner hour. The dishes are finally done and now you are going to take time to sit down for a while. The moment you land in the chair, two little ones are clinging to you wanting a story read to them. To make matters worse, you've read the story so many times you are absolutely bored all the way through. If forced to go a mile—then go two.

Steve did not realize how controlling he was of Carol. He was right about most things—at least in his eyes. He had expectations and these he clearly communicated. As the oldest of his brothers and sisters, he was in the habit of being responsible for them as well as ordering others around. The problem was that she likewise had two younger sisters whom she helped raise, and she felt more comfortable being the one in charge. He would tell her what to do and she somehow wouldn't get it done. He told her how much to spend on groceries and she would run over. He would be furious, but next week the drama was repeated. She would tell him to clean up the mess he made with his magazines and he would get really mad. She had no business telling him what to do. He was the head of the household. Any force she used on him elicited comments about how unbiblical and unspiritual she had become.

Their marriage grew more and more tense. He forced and she unconsciously fought back by conveniently forgetting or making mistakes. She forced and he retaliated with anger and guilt. Their marriage vacillated between a silent power struggle and loud war. Either way, the issue of who was forcing whom to do what became the focal point of their lives. The longer it went, the less willing either of them was to cooperate and do something the other wanted. Nobody would go even a quarter of a mile. They were locked into combat like two stags whose horns had become entangled so they couldn't disengage from their conflict. What does this produce? Certainly not a sense of freedom. It produces only captivity to one's own spirit and a relationship that is bound in a state of pressure.

It was not until later in life when the kids began leaving home that they were able to refocus on their relationship and begin to let go of their need to control. It was at this point that the relationship began to change, so they could begin to take on the characteristic Christ described.

Dealing with force from others on an emotional level produces many feelings that are from the archives of childhood. From about the age of two on, children are confronted with the awareness that others want something from them and they may well be forced into doing it. They react with resistance. *No* becomes a popular word in their vocabulary. In addition to their emotions, they begin to develop patterns for dealing with coercion in their lives. They can agree to accept parental force. This is considerably easier if the force is limited and expressed with concern for their well-being. When done with malice, hostility or as a put-down, the later repercussion is very great. Others learn that they can outsmart the parent and get around the issue. They become tricky and deceptive. When told he has to pick up his toys, he starts a fight with the baby and Mom forgets about his toys. Then there is little Susie who gets hurt and overwhelmed at the huge job of putting away all those toys. She cries and Mom feels guilty so she does it for her. Guess how Susie will handle her husband's force 20 years later? Other kids take the route of a direct refusal confrontation and simply out-bully the parent. All these primitive ways of dealing with force carry into marital patterns. The emotion behind them likewise carries forward. That is why some wives rebel in leftover anger or husbands collapse in hurt and withdrawal when forced. Power relationships, which are initially formed with parental figures, create a considerable amount of emotion.

An awareness of past feelings about power is important in being aware of what you do now as an adult when you are forced. Christ describes the Kingdom Life as being willing to go a second mile. This is not a display of weakness but is a powerful response of choice.

Questions for Discussion

1. What may be some reasons that people try to force others?

2. Jesus says when forced, do even more. Does this indicate a position of weakness? Inferiority?

3. Why does it show strength to do even more when being forced?

4. What happens to the person applying the force when you choose to do double what he is pressuring you into doing?

5. How do your family members force each other?

6. How do your family members deal with each other's forcefulness?

Matthew 5:42

Give to him who asks you, and from him who wants to borrow from you do not turn away.

9

Giving What Is Yours

Matthew 5:42

What is the value of things when you compare them to people? We are again confronted with Christ's value system which says that people and their needs are more important than things. In a society oriented toward acquisition as a way of confirming one's personal value, it makes little sense to give away your possessions. The act of eliminating possessions is, in some ways, descriptive of your own personal worth, if you agree that your value is based on what you own. Christ was not asking people to give up personal integrity. He was operating from a different value system. His system of values in the Kingdom was a different culture than the one to which you are accustomed. Why would Christ ask you to give up possessions? What happens in a relationship when one person takes something of personal value to himself and gives it to another person?

There needs to be an awareness when one gives as to what the effect will be on the other person, as well as one's own motivation. If you give him something so that you will be accepted, have you really given anything? There is also his own well-being to consider. By giving to certain people, you can destroy them. I recently saw a rather sad television commentary on a group of island people that the U.S. government decided to support because we had disrupted their lives by military activity. They had been people with dignity who were living vital lives. After years of supplying them with food, etc., they were lethargic, unemotional, and had lost their sense of vitality. We destroyed them. Giving can be very destructive when not done with wisdom. "It is better to give than to receive" literally deals with the way humans respond to receiving; receiving only can greatly destroy a person.

Therefore, in this principle in Matthew 5:42, I believe Christ would have you consider to whom you are giving and what it will do to them. He is saying—don't hang on to possessions but consider the well-being of others, which brings you back to the question of who owns possessions anyway.

Mark was often busy on Saturday for it was his day to mow the yard and catch up around the house. Also, because he and Christie were both busy with careers, they would frequently plan some special time together on Saturdays. Sometimes they went to the beach, other times just to a movie; but it was their day. He found, usually by Thursday, that he was mentally planning his Saturday and looking forward to a change in routine. However, one Saturday morning his co-worker from the office dropped over. He talked and talked. He was obviously lonely since his divorce a few months before. Mark grew more and more frustrated as it became less and less likely for him to fulfill his plans. He tried to listen to Jim but was really uninvolved. He was only being polite. Soon he found a way to get rid of Jim. Later, when discussing it with Christie who also had given up her morning, he realized what had happened, and then he felt somewhat guilty. Jim had asked for his day—Mark had put the lawn and work schedule ahead of him. Yet Jim was a person of more worth than what Mark had indicated to him by pushing him out the door.

Sometimes a person will ask for something, like time, without saying, "Can I have some of your time?" To be able to give to those who ask, you must be aware of how people go about asking. Some can be direct; others are demanding like a bull in a china shop. Others are so soft and vague that their request is barely audible. How does your wife ask you for things? How do your kids go about making requests? What signs are there in your husband when he wants something? How do you treat others who ask you for something?

Christ is presenting a principle in terms of letting go. Perhaps this is where spiritual growth really takes place. I am reminded again and again throughout Scripture that the more spiritually mature person is the one able to let go instead of acquiring and hanging on. Moses had to let go of a royal and palatial life-style to lead Israel. Noah let go of his status and acceptance in his community. Abraham had to let go of his son. Hannah had to let go of Samuel. When Jesus called His disciples they let go of their fishing business. Christ even asked a little boy to let go of his fish and loaves. Many are the examples of people who were willing to let go so that God could work and fulfill His purpose. On those occasions where people were unwilling to do so, the results were the opposite. Jonah was unwilling to let go of his life and go to Nineveh. The wealthy young man who came to Christ was apparently unable to let go of his wealth.

Christ told people that unless they were willing to give up their families and lands to follow Him, they would not be His disciples. Unless a grain of wheat falls into the ground and dies, it cannot produce wheat. I am not sure why we should be so puzzled by the idea that true life comes through letting go. Has not even your own life been designed as a process of letting go through aging? Sad are those who are aging but are unable to let go of some characteristic of youth. Yet no matter how hard they struggle, the aging process goes on. How much easier for those who can accept it and let go appropriately.

Perhaps people have bought a false bill of goods, thinking that freedom and the joy of living come through a process of acquiring and retaining. Does the man who is a millionaire have more or less freedom than the man who has little money? Because he has more, it is also more difficult to do what Christ is teaching here. This is why He says it is more difficult for a man with wealth to live a life in the Kingdom than for a camel to get through a needle's eye. It is easier to give what you have if you have little to lose.

A friend of mine who hitchhiked around the United States as a young man told me of the many kindnesses he experienced. People offered him places to stay, work, food, sometimes even money. The thing he noticed, however, was that the more generous offers came from people who had little. He could not understand this except, "I guess they didn't have much to lose—they could afford to be generous."

"Let go" is the principle Christ is teaching here. By hanging on to your things you cannot express the love that was at the base of all that Christ was teaching. You cannot find life by acquiring and hanging on to things.

The most extreme example of this I have ever heard of was in a newspaper article about a lady with a beautiful gold watch. She worried and worried that it would be stolen, so in order to gain release from her worry, she finally swallowed the watch. This way she felt she could preserve it safely and yet not worry. She was not exactly what I would call a free person. (Let's hope it was a Timex that could literally "take a licking and keep on ticking.")

Dr. Paul Tournier has noted that we cannot give that which we have not received. This attitude helps us to understand why it is difficult for those who have received little to be capable of giving a lot. Perhaps this is why someone who has an awareness of receiving everything from God is able to give more. It also means that the recipient is now potentially able to give to others. This act of giving to those who ask may well be the first link in a chain of reactions that carries to other people. What a model for your children to pass on to future generations.

Questions for Discussion

1. What considerations need to be made when someone asks you for something?

2. How can your freely giving to another person affect his giving to others?

3. What happens in our lives when we let go? What happens when we hold on?

4. In what ways has God given to us when we have made a request of Him? Can this be a model for us?

5. What are people in your family asking from you either verbally or nonverbally?

Matthew 5:42

Give to him who asks you, and from him who wants to borrow from you do not turn away.

10

Always a Lender Be
Matthew 5:42

If someone wants to borrow something from you, loan it to him. This principle is built essentially on the same premise as the previous one, except you retain ownership of your possession. People are more important than things. When you live in an industrial society where the whole focus is on production and profit, it is easy to be lulled into forgetting this. The industrial world we live in has so permeated our lives that our thinking is affected by it just by virtue of assimilation. We are bombarded hundreds of times a day with ads to get us to acquire things. The media is loaded with an emphasis on possessions. Whoever saw a billboard, paid for by an industry, that said, "Love your neighbor"? The usual message is clearly oriented to reflect the importance of things.

Even our architecture is designed to reflect the importance of things. Stores are designed to create an atmosphere in which we buy more. Industrialization is carried into design of schools. Our schools are essentially designed to look like factor-ies—perhaps reflecting the concept that they are stamping out a product.

We are so permeated by a production mentality that we have used industrial models to apply to our home life and churches. The administration of churches is often based on industrial models with boards taking control and running the programs, building bigger and better buildings, and even hir-ing staff whose time is consumed by managing property and starting more programs. In home life, our concept of the father as the head of the home often reflects a person who collects power and runs the show.

Christ, as the Head of the church, was fre-quently the opposite of this model. He dispensed power to others rather than collecting it to Him-self. We are given spiritual gifts and shall perform even greater miracles. People's worth in our soci-ety is measured by how many things they can accumulate. In this whole world system based on the importance of things, Christ says, "Lend that which you have."

The hesitancy to lend items to others has to do with the concept of loss. Suppose they break it or don't return it in usable condition? The decision to lend or not is often based on how valued the object is to the owner, as well as how responsible the borrower tends to be as a person. Could you stand to part with it? Lending based on whether or not you think you'll get the item back in good condition is not a concept taught by Christ. He simply says, "If somebody wants to borrow some-thing you own—lend it to him."

In fact, over in Luke 6:35, the Scripture says that when you lend you should do so without even expecting anything in return. Whether or not you get anything back is not the issue. The issue is meeting the needs of others. If you set high expectations on the returning, it may prove a frustrating experience for you. However, if you lend with the attitude that you may well not get anything in return, you prevent disappointment. This certainly has application with the lending of money as well as possessions.

I was talking with a pastor friend of mine about the church's ministry in the neighborhood. He related to me how recently a family, not from their church, had come to him explaining their need to borrow some folding tables. Their daughter was getting married. They had little money and wanted to have a reception in their backyard. His first thought was: *We cannot lend these tables out to people—the church needs them and suppose they get scratched or broken?* His initial reaction was a pleasant no. Then he began asking himself, *Why is this church in this neighborhood?* He concluded that since they were there to reach out to people, people were more important than tables. The tables were only a tool and now he had an opportunity, in Christian love, to meet some real needs. With this in mind, he readily agreed to lend the tables with no strings attached. It is hard for me to imagine Christ ever refusing to lend people any possession He had. So why is it then that people cling so much to that which they have?

Sometimes you focus on the possession and forget the people. What do you own that you are not willing to lend? What if your wife wants to use your new tennis racket when a friend invites her to play tennis? You know she can't swing straight and will scrape it on the cement. What if your daughter wants to borrow your new sweater? When your son wants to use your wrenches to fix his bike, are you thinking about your wrenches or your son? There are risks to loaning—your possessions may be broken or lost. To help your children learn to be responsible you should take time to see that they respect what they borrow. You may need to ask your son if he cleaned the wrenches and returned them to the garage. That means you must remember to check. The lending process now makes a demand on your time.

There are times when parents don't let children borrow something because they know they are not yet ready for the incumbent responsibility. You would not lend your car to your 15-year-old son just because he wants to drive it around the block. That is not what Christ is talking about; the principle is that you are to focus on the needs of the person rather than on your possessions. What was your response the last time one of your kids wanted to borrow something that belonged to you? Did you imply to them that you valued your possession more than their needs?

I wonder what Jesus would answer to the question, "How often should you lend things to people?" My guess is that He would respond similarly to the way He did when He was asked, "How many times should you forgive someone?" I don't hear Him setting limits so, therefore, I conclude the limits have to do with love. You should lend as long as it is in the best interest of the borrower.

This especially should apply to your family. In our culture we are very individualistically-oriented, rather than community-oriented. In some cultures, items essentially belong to everyone; they are viewed as common property. In these cultures, not giving access to items would not make any sense at all. In our culture, however, our identity is tied to that which we own. "Oh, I know you—you're the one who lives in the big white house at the end of the street." Even our children identify themselves by what they own. "My truck," "my doll," etc. become part of how they distinguish themselves from others in early development. What do we teach our children about lending to brothers and sisters? Are we teaching them to hoard possessions in adulthood or are we encouraging them to be lenders?

Questions for Discussion

1. What other biblical passages deal with the value of things compared to the value of people?

2. In what ways do we get acculturated into our world and its value system in lieu of being transformed?

3. If you lend something to a person and it comes back broken, how might you handle the situation with him?

4. What possessions do you feel good about loaning to family members and what possessions would you not want to loan? What determines the difference?

Matthew 5:43-48

You have heard that it has been said, "You shall love your neighbor and hate your enemy." But I say to you, love your enemies, bless those who curse you, do good to those who hate you, and pray for those who spitefully use you and persecute you, that you may be sons of your Father who is in heaven; for He makes His sun rise on the evil and on the good, and sends rain on the just and on the unjust. For if you love those who love you, what reward have you? Do not even the tax collectors do the same? And if you greet your brethren only, what do you do more than others? Do not even the tax collectors do so? Therefore you shall be perfect, just as your Father in heaven is perfect.

11

Eliminating Enemies
Matthew 5:43-48

How difficult can it get? Now look at what Jesus is asking of those who want to be His followers: "Love your enemies" (Matt. 5:44). Our enemy, by definition, is a person with whom we are fighting. So if we love him, what happens? He may well be hard pressed to continue his hatred and his battle. No doubt a number of enemies have been neutralized by being overpowered, but they may also be neutralized through being loved.

A few years ago the United States was going through the experience of having 52 of our citizens held captive by Iran. The hostages were being mistreated and abused emotionally. Although I believed the issues were more complex than what met the eye, I found myself angry over what was occurring. Iran became our enemy. One day in the midst of my frustration and anger, I was struck by an article entitled, "Iran—Maybe We Should Just Ask Them to Forgive Us." It reminded me again of what Christ was saying: "If you love only those who love you, that is nothing. Even the crooked and despised tax collectors do that" (5:46).

Here He is calling us to love our enemies. Are we to take Him literally or is He just making statements for people to think about in a more general fashion? When you consider other aspects of what He is saying in this passage, it is difficult not to take Him literally. He instructs us to pray for those who persecute us. He does not mean to pray for their demise, and I am not completely convinced that He even means to pray for them to quit persecuting us. I believe He means to pray for their well-being. He follows this with an example of how God the Father relates to these awful people who are busy hurting us. God expresses love for them by making His sun to shine on them and by sending them rain. I assume that, in an agricultural economy, this would be somewhat akin to prospering them. I, however, often see Christians just delighting in the idea that God is going to zap anyone who crosses them or is mean to them. They believe God is a big brother who will beat up anybody that picks on them. I recall hearing one pastor trying to convince his congregation of his good rapport with God by telling how one of his staff members at a former church gave him a bad time and then suddenly died. Hardly does God confirm that concept in this passage. In fact, Jesus even goes on to say that He sees no reason at all why any Christian should be rewarded spiritually if he doesn't love his enemy. Furthermore, He says that if we are going to be like God we need to be mature enough to do this. Perhaps this is a part of growing up into Him.

So what does all of this have to do with your family life today and tomorrow? It depends on how you define an enemy. I must say I have seen innumerable families battling in such a way that they looked more like enemies than friends. There are times when husband/wife, parent/child, brothers/sisters set out intending to inflict pain or even seeking to destroy each other emotionally if not physically. These times of enmity may be periodic reactions to some point of pain or threat, or they could be more of an ongoing relationship related to a continuous state of bitterness or hatred. Certainly there are times when people flare up in a moment of anger, and later look back with regret. Christ is saying when your wife, who knows you are sensitive about being a failure, gets angry and points out that you're a terrible husband, you still love her. She knew the location of the soft vulnerable underbelly and drove the knife into that spot, but you still love her. When your husband knows that you fear rejection, yet he comes into the room and withholds himself from relating, you love him rather than attack.

But what do you do with all your anger at being called a failure or being rejected? Do you stuff that all inside? Certainly not! Those feelings need to be dealt with; but better that you work through those feelings of anger with a spouse who is a friend and not an enemy.

We were discussing the war going on in their home. Intellectually, she could see what was happening. The two of them had gone away for a weekend together. En route, he began to condemn her for everything in the book. She took the bait and counterattacked—the pattern was clear. This was their second marriage and both were afraid to get too close to each other emotionally. As soon as they felt this happening, they would begin a distancing process. A weekend away together was risky. What if they got too close emotionally? If they did, and something happened to the relationship, they would really hurt. Neither wanted to be hurt like that again, yet each desired closeness. She could understand but invariably she found herself attacking back. "Why do I get so caught up in his process—I can't let him condemn me." Together by attack and counterattack, they stayed distant.

The first step in not reacting to being attacked by a family member is to be aware of *why* you're reacting. What are you trying to prove and to whom? What are the feelings you haven't dealt with from the past that get involved?

We have previously discussed anger and some of its dynamics. Certainly you may feel anger, but categorizing your spouse or child as an enemy, so that you can retaliate and feel self-righteous in the process of so doing, cannot be substantiated by this teaching. To love your enemy does not mean that you do not confront him with what you feel he is doing to you that's painful. It does mean that you confront in ways that are not destructive to him as a person. When unfairly condemned, you don't try to kill him with kindness. You do not say to yourself, *I have this clever plan. Every time my husband criticizes me, I will simply hold my tongue and when he is finished I will give him a kiss.* This may not be at all loving your enemy. It may rather be only a strategy for outflanking your enemy so you can ward off his anger. It does not show any concern for his personhood. The focus is on protecting yourself. The concept of loving your enemy has to do with concern for him, rather than protecting yourself by keeping him from attacking or hurting.

Why do this? Why should anyone love his enemy? By virtue of categorization, whenever anyone is labeled, there is no way of reaching him or relating to him in love. He is relegated to a group of people that you mistreat or mistrust in whatever way you want. For some reason, we human beings frequently evaluate people in terms of in-groups or out-groups. If people are like us, they are in; if not like us we condemn them. Are they Baptists, hippies, Democrats, motorcyclists, Southerners, carpenters, men, golfers, working mothers, or prostitutes? Depending on our own perspective as to what all those categories mean, we either treat people kindly or push them aside and reject them. If they are not like us, they can easily be categorically judged and condemned, but not seen as people. The category of *enemy* is the most conspicuous and easiest to utilize. Once we label someone as enemy, our obligations to love him cease.

Husband and wife are to love each other even while being besieged by each other. Parents are to love their children even when those kids are doing hurtful things toward them. This may not be as difficult as meets the eye, because you already have great attachment and involvement with your enemy. You become intimate with both those you love and those who are your enemies.

Enemies are then seen as being totally without value and should rightly be eliminated; eliminated as enemies, but preserved as persons worthy of love. I think of our position spiritually and the love of God that cuts through that enemy category rather than discarding the person because of it. It is while we were yet sinners and living in opposition to God that Christ died for us. He did not categorize us as enemies and, as a consequence, withdraw from loving us.

How can it be possible to love someone who is hurting you? Certainly this goes against your very nature. It is through the internalization of the love that you have received that you can in turn love someone who is being unkind or causing you to suffer. This passage deals with the concept that you are to be like Christ and different from others. If you love your enemies, do you not think you would be like a light shining on a hill? It's a very salty way of life. When you think of the actual experience of this life-style you can understand why a Christian is known by his love. If you love only as others do, nobody knows you are a Christian. It takes a more radical love. Too often those who are Christians are condemned because they don't show up for every church service, give enough money, study the Bible enough, attend midweek prayer service. Interestingly, I don't recall ever hearing another Christian condemned or judged because he didn't love his enemy enough.

Recently I was talking with a friend, John, who loves his children very much. His son was very distressed because his skateboard was missing and the other kids said that a neighbor boy had taken it. The father went to the boy's home and asked him about the skateboard and, of course, the boy denied knowing anything about it. John, knowing he was being lied to, asked the boy if he had a skateboard of his own. The boy said that he did not have one. John told the boy he could understand him wanting one if he didn't have one. Although John has only a modest income, he took his last five dollars out of his pocket and gave it to the boy. He said that he wanted to be the first to contribute to his getting a skateboard. With that he assumed the matter was closed. He had loved his enemy. The next morning the doorbell rang. He opened the door to find the boy and his father—with the missing skateboard. They wanted to talk to him and to return his son's skateboard.

On another occasion, John's daughter had candy taken away from her by some older kids on the block. At first my friend was furious. Then he took daughter in hand and returned to the store. He purchased a bag of candy and set out in the car to locate the older girls. Upon finding them, he confronted them—in love—with what they had done and the inappropriateness of their behavior. After that, he gave them the bag of candy. Since that time they have never once bothered his daughter and, in fact, every time they see him they wave and talk with him. He has an open relationship with them.

Both of these situations turned out well. But even if they had not, it would not have mattered. John had lived his life with others in a way he felt was consistent with the teachings of Christ, rather than consistent with his human nature. These principles work in breaking down barriers between people. Living this out with your family, however, should be the result of love rather than some manipulative way to get skateboards returned.

Christ is talking about a new way to treat others—even when they are hurting you. This is not without a cause or purpose. If you desire to be like Christ, the motivation should be strong, for He talks about loving your enemies as a way of demonstrating that you are His child. This assumes that children behave like their parents.

Living this kind of love also requires great faith, faith that God will supply your needs and care for you rather than you being able to overpower your enemy in your strength. Even the Proverbs tell us that, although it is men who prepare the horses for battle, it is God who grants the victory (Prov. 21:31).

When a close friend was going through a divorce, her husband took the papers to his attorney in order to settle the estate. She decided in faith she would do that which she believed God would have her do and, with an "If I perish, I perish" attitude she proceeded. Years later, her husband decided he would force her to sell the home she and the children were living in because he wanted his share of the money to support his new loose life-style. When her attorney reviewed the paperwork he could not believe the contract was drawn by her husband's attorney. The entire agreement was drawn in such a way that she could not be displaced. The agreement completely protected her and the kids' best interest.

To be able to be a child of God in loving an enemy, we must have the faith to believe that God will not allow us to be destroyed in the process.

Questions for Discussion

1. What would motivate Jesus to ask you to love your enemies?

2. What part does faith play in loving your enemies?

3. Is it possible to consistently live a life that goes against our human nature?

4. What are the options that confront an enemy who has received love in return for pain?

5. How can you express love toward your spouse the next time he/she intentionally hurts you?

Matthew 6:1-4

Take heed that you do not do your charitable deeds before men to be seen by them. Otherwise you have no reward from your Father who is in heaven. Therefore, when you do a charitable deed, do not sound a trumpet before you as the hypocrites do in the synagogues and in the streets, that they may have glory from men. Assuredly, I say to you, they have their reward. But when you do a charitable deed, do not let your left hand know what your right hand is doing, that your charitable deed may be in secret; and your Father who sees in secret will Himself reward you openly.

12

To Thyself—Honor and Glory

Matthew 6:1-4

Your actions have no lasting value if you do them with the motive that other people will look at you and marvel at how great you are. If you are going to express love for your family, do not do it with the idea that they will look at you with more respect, think that you are a super parent or love you more for it. Christ is calling to our attention that it is not only your behavior that has value, it is also the motive behind the behavior. When a person sets out to express some set of behavior because he wants to be like Christ, it is different than doing it in order to gain recognition and praise from others.

How many times do you do things for your husband because you want to show him what a great wife you are? It is not terrible that you want to be a great wife. But when you go out of your way to fill the car with gas because you want to impress your husband, you are doing it for yourself and not for him. When you bring your wife some flowers because she will tell her friends about the wonderful thing that you have done and they will think that you are the most thoughtful husband in the world—you have your reward! When you take the kids to the amusement park and load them with Cokes and popcorn in order to guarantee their love for you—you are attempting to misuse your assets for selfish purposes.

Why is it that people will give alms to impress others? Why will they pray ostentatious prayers to gain attention? Perhaps it is part of human nature to want to be loved, respected, valued, appreciated. Some theorists believe that people have a drive to be respected just as they have a drive for food and shelter. The problem is that your relationship to God, as well as to your family members, can be disrupted by this drive to be "respected." When a person sets out to elevate himself rather than to love, he is isolated in his attention and cannot relate. He cannot live with another in an "I-thou" relationship because he is busy trying to live above others.

What happens in families when people are motivated to do things so that they will be noticed? Sue could list for him everything she had ever done for him during the past 20 years. Furthermore, she frequently kept Paul updated on the list. She had cooked for him, gone on vacations where he wanted, not yelled when he bought a fishing boat, and had even helped clean his smelly fish. Daily, new items were added to the list. She especially enjoyed the ones that were very self-sacrificing because they were worth at least triple value. It was obvious that she was functioning as the perfect wife out of a desire to honor herself. She kept a close tally on the score and was constantly reminding him. How could Paul fault her for anything after she had done so much for him over the years? The question was, had she really done all those wonderful things for him? If it's done to continue the "I do more around here than you" contest, it will likely be ineffective in the long run. This becomes only one-upmanship which has nothing to do with living a life consistent with God's Kingdom.

The kids couldn't wait until Saturday. Mom and Dad were taking them to Disneyland. They were delighted to be going. However, the oldest daughter felt a twinge of guilt. There had been lots of talk about Disneyland since her best friends had gone last month. Mom and Dad were reluctant to go at first because the electric bill was due and the credit card charges were peaking out at their limit. Yet, older sis had more experience with her mom and dad than the other two. Mom and Dad had told them that they would go, but they would have to wait until summer when there would be more money in the bank. But—she did not want to wait. She clearly pointed out that her friends' parents took the time and money to take their children to Disneyland and besides—since both of them were working now she was feeling ignored and neglected. There was even a slight hint that she would not like them if they didn't cooperate. She knew all the right buttons to push. Mom and Dad now felt pressured to show everybody that they were good parents; so they buckled under the pressure and decided to go. Their motive was to prove to themselves and to others that they were okay. They needed to be the model of good parents and not risk loss of respect. They did not take the kids because they loved them and wanted to express the love by seeing them enjoy themselves. They went because they felt they had to prove something about themselves.

The principle taught in this section (Matt. 6:1-4) of Christ's discourse is this: you need to do good deeds to others out of love, not to receive recognition. This is particularly difficult for those who are raised in homes where the family focuses on what other people will think. Do you drive the right car? Do you wear the right clothes? Do you have the right successes? Your worth and value are based on performance. The other group of people who struggle with this area are those who grow up in homes where they did not feel accepted. When the need for acceptance is not met, many of them spend a lifetime of sensitivity, riveted to observing how well others are accepting them. It can become the focal point in their lives. They expend great energy trying to impress others favorably in order to be accepted. This does not allow them the time or energy to be busy in secretly loving others.

Let me give you an example of a marriage in which there was much conflict. This was the second marriage for both of them. They both had children which was also a source of stress. She had tried and tried to work on their relationship. She herself was a child who had lost her mother. She had a stepmother to whom she felt very unacceptable. As we were talking one afternoon in one of our sessions, with tears streaming down her cheeks she confided, "I must show him that I am a lovable person. I must prove it to him." I responded, "To whom are you trying to prove this?" At that point a light seemed to come into her eyes and I could see that she was beginning to understand that the things she was doing were designed to get a response of love in order that she could prove to herself that she was acceptable and lovable. In spite of all her words to the contrary, she really was not at all convinced that she was an acceptable person. Her behavior was great, but her motive had to do with her own needs and not with his.

We forget that we really do spend a great deal of time deceiving ourselves. The response of a person living in the Kingdom is that he secretly does loving things for his family without letting anyone know. Perhaps it is the extra care in preparing his lunch—he may never know that you gave him the last cupcake and that you did without.

Perhaps it is taking the time to pick up your shoes from the living room floor even when your wife doesn't see you do it. Maybe it is setting Junior's bike in out of the rain or picking up Sister's doll from the hallway where everyone is stepping on it rather than around it. Maybe it is taking the family to Disneyland just because you can observe their thrill, even when you don't need them to be thrilled.

Questions for Discussion

1. When we express love by our actions in a very obvious way, what is our reward?

2. Can you really learn much about people by observing their actions or do you also need to know the context of the action?

3. When a loving deed is done with the intent that others will give us honor for it, is it really love?

4. What happens to a relationship where an act of love is performed in order to bring self-glorification?

5. Does receiving honor for something you have done always have a negative impact on your life?

6. How have you secretly expressed love to each family member? How about in the past week?

Matthew 6:14,15

For if you forgive men their trespasses, your heavenly Father will also forgive you. But if you do not forgive men their trespasses, neither will your Father forgive your trespasses.

13

Measuring Forgiveness
Matthew 6:14,15

What part does forgiveness play in the life of a person who is living the Kingdom Life? In Matthew 6:14,15 it is apparent that forgiveness is a reflection of the Christian life-style. Here it is presented in a way that may seem like a threat from God; but this interpretation—"If you don't forgive others, God won't forgive you"—seems to be out of context with the character of God. Perhaps Matthew 6:14,15 is not so much a threat as it is a principle of God's relationship to mankind. It may be that it is similar to "whosoever believes on Him, shall have eternal life." In this sense it becomes a principle but also describes a way of life: "Since God has forgiven you, you forgive those around you."

I find it interesting that Christ addresses this issue in the context of describing those who do all the right things for the wrong motives and are in all the right places for all the wrong people's benefit. Christ is talking about false relationships. He has just finished talking about praying in such a fashion as to be the best performer in town, and then He follows by describing a man putting on a false face when fasting. Basically He is describing deception in relationships. People are putting on spiritual masks in order to be highly regarded by others. One can see them trying to gain a sense of deep respect from others. But they do not have a genuine concern for their relationship with God. They are using their relationship with God in an effort to impress those around them.

In the midst of this discourse, Jesus tells His followers to be forgiving. Perhaps a person's spiritual maturity can be more accurately measured by how forgiving he is rather than by the amount of religious symbolism with which he surrounds himself.

Within the family unit, people are sometimes shocked to find that they are living with other human beings rather than the angelic beings they had dreamed them to be. They grow to know one another well, both in terms of their holiness and their humanness. It is within this living system that forgiveness is frequently needed. Not just forgiveness in the sense of the words "I forgive you," but in terms of spiritual and emotional attitude toward the other persons. It does not mean that you will forget the hurt or pain you suffered at the hands of another. It does mean that it is no longer an emotionally-charged issue. It is the difference between touching an electrical wire that is connected, and touching one that is not connected.

Larry and Pam had a basically good marriage and their two girls were doing well in their growth and development. Larry came home right on time this particular day and was pleased to be greeted by everyone. After dinner he decided to work in the yard for a little while. Pam had secretly hoped that they could spend some time talking and gave him a disgusted look as he went out the door, yet she didn't say a word. This look caught him in a painful area of his life. He had often felt like he let his mother down when he was a kid because she had essentially controlled him by guilt. Larry left the room without a word—he could not be controlled. He was angry, but from previous arguments he knew that if he said anything Pam would retreat by saying, "Why are you so upset? I didn't say you couldn't work in the yard."

He worked until after dark that night, mostly to avoid her. Besides, she had put him down by her look of disgust and he was angry. When he entered the kitchen, he didn't bother to remove the mud on his shoes. When Pam saw the mud she remarked coldly, "You tracked in mud." His response of "oh, it must have been from my working in our yard" did little to conceal his anger. Neither of them would give an inch. In some ways they had decided together to not deal with their feelings. Both became so locked in to their own anger, they continued through the evening without talking. Finally, the next day at breakfast, she opened up the issue—she usually had the role in the family of calling off the fights. "Are you still angry?" she asked. He knew, from their repeated pattern of disagreements and reconciliations, that this was the cue. He was then able to express himself and reveal his hurt feelings from her angry look. She was able then to ask for his forgiveness. They hugged and made up, and the emotional charge that had built up now served to propel them together again. They each felt exhilaration where there had once been a heavy weight.

They had each secretly battled for control. The battle ended when she gave in by opening up the conversation. But they were not aware of that issue just yet. They were too relieved of tension to press further into the dynamics of their marriage. This is typical of the little forgiveness issues that daily confront families. There are also the long-term issues that come from bigger problems. These issues carry over time and become like an incessant arthritic pain that one cannot seem to alleviate. That affair that he had in the third year of their 17-year marriage; the time she walked out and left him; their difficult relationship with her parents—all are examples of deeper, long-term hurts that haunt a marriage in which there is no forgiveness. Recently a wife expressed to me the impact in their marriage from a situation in her husband's childhood. His mother had won a beauty contest just prior to discovering her pregnancy with him. When she was required to relinquish her crown, she was never able to forgive her baby. Her lack of forgiveness impacted his relationship with his mother throughout his entire childhood, and now was impacting his relationship with his wife.

How do you know that your life reflects the character of God? You will know it when there is forgiveness in the ebb and flow of your daily life. It does not mean that your spouse or your children have not deeply hurt you; it means that you no longer hold that against them. Without forgiveness, you become bitter in life, bitter in your family life, bitter with your friends. You are like a lake with no outlet into which flows the hurt and pain of life. After a time of no resolution, your focus in life is on the bitter rather than the joyful experiences. Without forgiveness, you will drift into a focus on yourself and your right to feel sorry for yourself because of the terrible way others treat you. There is little room for looking at your process of collecting hurt rather than forgiving. Likewise there is little room left to love others.

I do not recall ever seeing families that are vital, healthy, and growing if forgiveness is not an active part of their family life. It is difficult to request forgiveness when one interprets it as a sign of weakness rather than strength. Likewise, it is difficult if it is misconstrued to mean "and furthermore, I'll never hurt you again." When a person asks for forgiveness it does not mean that he will never repeat that which has offended you. It is no guarantee of safety from hurt.

There are situations where the words "please forgive me" are abused because they are not sincere. They are designed to ward off the spouse's anger or to appease him. Therefore, this most important aspect of relationship needs to be understood and practiced in the true sense of forgiveness which Christ modeled. It is to be freely given even when not asked for. It means being willing to let go of a hurt or an emotional "I owe you." The debt to you is cancelled.

Questions for Discussion

1. Can forgiving someone be an act of worship? If so, in what sense?

2. What characteristics must a person have if he is going to forgive you?

3. How can you tell if someone has forgiven you?

4. What happens in a person's life when he refuses to forgive others?

5. Are there people within your immediate or extended family whom you have never been able to forgive for something?

6. What are the difficult areas for you to forgive in others?

7. Is there anything so terrible that Christ would not forgive?

Matthew 6:19-21

Do not lay up for yourselves treasures on earth, where moth and rust destroy and where thieves break in and steal; but lay up for yourselves treasures in heaven, where neither moth nor rust destroys and where thieves do not break in and steal. For where your treasure is, there your heart will be also.

14

Storing Up Your Assets

Matthew 6:19-21

When you take away all the glitter and glamour of life, where is the meaning of life to be found—in things or in people? We all know how to expend our lives trying to store up treasures on earth. Yet we are surprised if we are the victims of crime, bad business cycles, or if inflation breaks through and steals. In spite of our investments of time, worry, and money to protect that which we have accumulated, loss still happens. We shouldn't be surprised because we have been told that these things will happen. Christ never spent much time out of His life having to paint the hull of His yacht, paying docking fees, earning money to buy insurance, applying for a license, worrying about a lawsuit, or purchasing padlocks. This verse does not make a whole lot of sense to those of us raised in a culture that says our value and worth are based on accumulation of possessions, stocks, and money-market funds. If our lives become dull because of all the pressures of living, a "successful" person can go and buy some fun, take a pleasure trip, and forget all the pressures.

Christ says, "Do not lay up for yourselves treasures" (Matt 6:19). He sent His disciples out to minister without their wallets, credit cards—or even a Samsonite suitcase full of clothes. Does that sound different than the manner in which His disciples operate today?

So how do you go out this week and lay up for yourself treasures in heaven? To answer this, one must ask, "What treasure will be found in heaven?" "What are these treasures that one should be laying in store?" People are in heaven! The treasure He is talking about is *people*. He seems to be saying, "Don't invest yourself in accumulating things, but invest yourself in people."

This winter our family visited a castle in California. The wealth was staggering—statuary from Europe, antiques hundreds of years old, gold-leafed ceilings in the guest house, ancient tapestries. There was even a workman whose full-time job was to haul ice to the polar bear each day. (I never did understand how one could feel fulfilled with a lifetime spent taking ice to a polar bear!) Yet I realized that the great man who built the castle and acquired the wealth of furnishings it contained—he who had achieved so much in his lifetime, still had to face death. Then of what use and meaning were all the things he spent a lifetime building? We cannot relate to his wealth, yet I see many businessmen who are very busy working their lives away to develop treasures—and the "tomorrow" they are going to spend with their wives and families never comes.

One weekend at a retreat I talked with a young couple. He introduced me to his wife who was polite, but obviously unresponsive to him. She soon walked away from our conversation. He explained to me that she was leaving him. He had been highly successful in his business and had acquired a lovely home, expensive cars and the "good life." He also had monthly expenses to keep up with all of it. When they married a few years earlier, he started out working 80 to 90 hours a week. Now he had made it big, but she was lost in the process. Her leaving was bringing his world in on top of him. "What can I do? Where do I go from here when she leaves in a couple of weeks?"

Many people get caught in the web of the pursuit of treasure and the more they struggle, the deeper they become entrapped. I do not recall anyone who has ever said, "Enough! I do not want or need any more money." I do not doubt that, shortly after his wife leaves, our young man will remarry. And within a couple of years he will be back making much income again. Life will return to a stabilized pursuit. Yet life does end, and then comes the confrontation with the reality of how that life was spent.

I contrast this with the life of my uncle who was killed in an auto accident recently. He never went to college, never had much income, never held an office in the community, never was prominent nor famous. However, he was a Christian, and his life reflected his faith. He was generous, he was kind, he cared about people and expressed his care to those whose lives crossed his on a daily basis. I talked to one of his sons by phone following the funeral. He told me that the family had gone to the funeral home the first night of the viewing. Even though it was a weeknight they expected a few people would come to express their care and concern. That night over 500 people made their way through those doors, and the following nights were similar. The family was more than overwhelmed as they realized how much this man had reached out to other people and influenced their lives. He had spent his life laying up treasures in heaven, as mirrored by the response to his death.

When Bill and Sue were young they dreamed of the day when they could get ahead and then take it easy. They started while their kids were still young, planning and working to give their kids more. Bill worked long days and in a few years had it all together. Sue worked too, and being bright, her career also advanced. Soon they had their dream house, two new cars, a large retirement account, and things were going well. They were seldom able to take a vacation with the kids because they both couldn't get the time off. But maybe he had a business trip by himself and could take a break at the hotel, or Sue would be off to a conference in Hawaii. Underneath they knew they were drifting apart, but by running faster they avoided dealing with that fact.

Soon the kids were teenagers. My, it seemed that just yesterday they were toddlers. They learned to be independent. They were good kids. The family went to church services most Sundays, so the kids had good input spiritually. They were given piano lessons and sent to Little League and gymnastics.

Now Bill and Sue were both in their late fifties. The children were married and there were grandchildren. Bill was told that the cancer was a slow one so he probably had a few more years. And now for the first time, realizing that he was not immortal, Bill was taking stock of his life, assessing what he had really achieved. He had always wanted to leave his mark on the world. Tomorrow it would be all over—then what? What "treasures" had he laid up in heaven?

Whenever you become "successful" and have many possessions, the question then becomes whether you own them or they own you. The time and effort needed to care for treasures you have acquired means time and resources which are drawn inward. Many successful people run faster each day to keep up with the new needs of their treasures. They must work now to care for, store, protect, and conserve them. When do they have time to invest in people?

People are more valuable than things. They need to be encouraged. They need the opportunity to grow spiritually and emotionally. They need the opportunity to interact with others' spiritual gifts, on both the giving and receiving aspects. Relationships take time. I am convinced that there is no way possible to help people grow without logging significant amounts of time with them. And the more treasures one has on earth the less time there is to spend with others.

Christ tells us what not to do, and then He tells us what we are called to achieve. He sets up a dichotomy: "Do not use your time acquiring things; use your time with others." He then goes on to talk of what happens to us when this is done. "Where a man's treasure is there will his heart be also" (Matt. 6:21). That is where he will focus his life. Sometimes people ignore Scripture and rationalize their life-style to themselves. "I can lay up treasures and still not get caught up in them." They believe that the money doesn't really mean that much to them. What they ignore is that slowly they fall in love with money and develop an emotional attachment to it. Christ tells us that years later the love for the money will be there.

Another aspect of investing in treasure on earth is that it has a way of blunting one's sensitivity to the needs of others. Christ could relate to those with whom He spent His time because He lived in their world. He knew what it meant to be without home or food. When people focus the meaning and purpose of their lives on things, it is difficult to feel compassion for the needs of those around them. When you are comfortable financially, how do you bring yourself to consider or to understand the mother in the inner city who can barely get through the week, or the elderly person struggling to live on a pension? How often do you think of them or feel with them? I dare say that most of us wrap ourselves in the cocoon of our comfortableness and seldom expose ourselves to those in great need.

Certainly this has application to marriages and families. The husband does not know his wife because he focuses on his treasure-accumulation plan. The children are treated as if they are in last place, behind Dad's and/or Mom's job. Their worth and value are greatly affected. Living the Kingdom Life means that a person is focused on others and not on wealth. Those around us can tell where our treasure is. We can verbalize an interest in people, but since we get drawn into the emotional investment, our real intent shows through to those around us. The Proverbs describe this: "Beware of stingy people, because they will invite you to dinner and tell you to eat, but they don't really mean it" (Prov. 23:7). One gets the sense that these stingy people are so caught up in what they have, that they cannot truly give to others. Even when they make attempts to be giving, it just doesn't work for them. They are not living in the Kingdom. They have eyes to see, but do not see that the Kingdom of God consists of *people* and not *things*.

Christ goes on to say to us in this case you can't have the best of both worlds. It will not work to try to serve both God and Money. You must choose which value system you want to set your life upon. He then, by using the birds and the flowers, points out the evidences of His care. All around you can see the proof of God's promise to take care of His own. It is our lack of faith, not God's lack of provision, that causes us to strive to accumulate. In our own society, acquisition of treasures has become an attempt to be self-reliant, to be hedonistic, to be somebody "important," to have respect and recognition. Are these not further attempts to provide for ourselves what God has already provided? These attempts, in turn, make family life difficult as well as make spiritual growth virtually impossible.

Where does your own family come into this decision of "life focus"? Are you expending your life with your spouse along with others? Do your children really know you? Do they know what is happening in your life? Do you know them? Do you know what they are worried about, what they are dealing with, what they are dreaming about? As one author so capably stated, "You should have your fingerprints all over the souls of those in your family."

Questions for Discussion

1. What does Christ say about life focus?

2. If He says that you cannot serve both God and money why did He allow some Old Testament leaders to be wealthy?

3. If you set out to lay up treasures on earth, what impact does this have on you spiritually? What impact does this have on your family? What happens if you succeed?

4. What would you do tomorrow if your assignment for the day was to lay up for yourself treasures in heaven?

5. How does laying up treasures in heaven affect family relationships?

6. Do you know any wealthy friends? How is their life different than it would be if they had no wealth?

Matthew 7:1-6

Judge not, that you be not judged. For with what judgment you judge, you will be judged; and with the same measure you use, it will be measured back to you. And why do you look at the speck that is in your brother's eye, but do not consider the plank that is in your own eye? Or how can you say to your brother, "Let me take the speck out of your eye"; and look, a plank is in your own eye? You hypocrite! First remove the plank from your own eye, and then you will see clearly to take the speck out of your brother's eye. Do not give what is holy to the dogs; nor cast your pearls before swine, lest they trample them under their feet, and turn and tear you in pieces.

15

Here Comes the Judge

Matthew 7:1-6

"You are constantly taking Brenda's side instead of mine!"

"Well, I don't know who to believe. You tell me one thing and she tells me another."

"I am your wife. Don't you realize what that means?"

"You sure don't act like a wife or you wouldn't be yelling at me all the time."

"Well, if you acted more like a husband instead of a child I wouldn't have to yell at you."

On and on they went. Their lives a steady flow of judging the other. Judgment followed by condemnation. Attack followed by counterattack.

"Do not judge others, lest you be judged by the same standards" (see Matt. 7:1). One of the most frequent phenomena I hear in talking with couples about their marriages is their judgment of, and desire to change, their spouses. Whenever there is stress in the relationship, the first assumption is that as soon as the spouse changes the marriage will be fine. They know *exactly* what is wrong with the spouse and what he/she needs to do to improve. They often seem somewhat startled or at a loss for words when asked what they perceive as their contributing part in the conflict. One of the first big hurdles in counseling is to help people to accept responsibility for their own feelings. There is often resistance to any change by either spouse.

In fact, there is a tendency to want to elicit the support of others (particularly authority figures) to join in the judging and condemning process. A person feels more secure when others join with him in judging. Then he *really* knows he is correct!

Rendering judgment has become a favorite pastime for families. I recently attended a lecture by a prominent family-life expert from a local university. He reported on a study done by a group of students in Florida in which they visited homes and counted the number of negative and positive interactions between parents and children. The study was done in average homes. They discovered that, with this group, 80 percent of the interactions were negative and only 20 percent were positive. Much judgment presented in negative ways permeates family life.

How do you relate to those within your family who judge you? (Everyone has been through the process of being on the receiving end of judgment.) Your personality closes down. You become rigid and closed off from others. You may become hurt or defensive. Another thing that happens is that in your defensiveness you start to judge others. All of these options cut off the relationship with the other person. When you reach the point where you can envision what judgment does to you and to others, you are better able to understand why judgment destroys love in relationships.

Perhaps the passage has a broader context than what first meets the eye. We are told that God will judge us with the same standards we use to judge others. Does this imply a threat from God? "I'll do to you what you are doing to others." Again, this seems out of character with God. Is He only a responder who does to us whatever we do first? It seems to me that this passage refers to a wider principle of relationships rather than a blunt threat by God. He has told us that we should serve Him out of love and not out of fear of retaliation. Perhaps Matthew 7:1 is saying that God's system is to consider each individual in light of his own method of relating to others. However, it may be seen more extensively in terms of a principle: the way you go about judging others is likely to be the way you will be considered by them.

I once had a client, an openly hostile man, who spent a great deal of time yelling and cursing at his wife. He attempted to get an understanding of why his wife was belligerent and was threatening to leave him. As we discussed what feelings he was prompting in her, he recalled a saying they had on the streets of New York where he had grown up. "What goes around, comes around." He could see the principle of "that which we give out will likely be returned again to us." If you give out love, you will find love is returned. If you give out judgment, you can well expect to receive judgment in return.

Christ is saying that we are judged again with the same judgment we give out. You were not called into this world to be a judge; you were called to love your neighbor as yourself. We are not taught that "people will know you (are a Christian) by your judgmentalness"!

He goes on to emphasize the extreme importance of self-awareness. You are not able to look at or correct a fault in your brother until you have corrected the faults that are in your own life. Once you can look upon your own faults, you are humbled to the point where you can help your brother. Then, however, your help will not come from judgment but from understanding. This passage compares a log to a speck. When you are aware of how unkind or insensitive you can be toward your wife, it does not seem like such a big deal when one day she snaps back at you. After you realize that you have not spent much time with your kids all week, their misbehavior can be understood as a tool to gain your attention.

Being a judgmental person brings about separation in the relationship. You are no longer living *with* the other person; you are living *above* him. The sense of oneness in the family is broken. People are being hurt from the aloofness as well as the condemnation. We tend to think that if we judge our spouse and condemn him/her, it will cause him/her to change or to improve. Think about that for a moment. How many times have you ever seen someone change for the better because another person was pounding away at him? I do not think that much change comes from being judged. I see it producing stubbornness, hurt, anger, rebellion—but I do not see much permanent change. Permanent change comes from response to love in the same way that Christ teaches that *our* lives are changed in response to *His* love.

Judgment has a way of dividing people into in-groups and out-groups, or acceptable and unacceptable people. Once you have judged and separated, those in the out-group cannot be reached spiritually nor emotionally by you.

Why do people judge? Undoubtedly for a variety of reasons. Those who were judged frequently by their parents will in turn judge their spouses and their own children in a similar fashion. It has become a way of life—a way of relating to other people. Even when they determine that they won't be judgmental, they find themselves judging others unless they get some help to change.

Others are judgmental as a way of trying to feel better about themselves. If you put everyone else down and focus on their faults, you don't feel so badly about yourself. It is a form of self-elevation by repressing others.

In a related sense, judgmentalism can be a way of dealing with your own faults. When you see your faults reflected back to you in the lives of others, you can condemn them. The things that you judge others for often have specific meaning to you in relation to your own life. Either you have been hurt by a parent or someone else in your childhood, or you see something that you detest in yourself but have never admitted. I recall a tract that I received once that was a ripping condemnation of television and the lewdness seen on it. The interesting thing about the tract, however, was the picture of Adam and Eve on the cover, their nude bodies barely covered by a few fig leaves.

Sometimes people have so much hostility within that it just keeps flowing out like a river. Anyone in their paths becomes the target. Often there is also an element of condemnation and anger at themselves as well. They judge other people in order to relieve their pent-up emotions and pressure. Like a cup overflowing into a saucer, those closest receive the greatest overflow of anger. The relief, unfortunately, only serves to reinforce further judgment.

They had come to me for counseling because of very verbal and sometimes physical fights. She was really angry at him because he was so "unreasonable, undependable, and unreliable." He was gone much of the time or would be late coming home from work. And when he was home he would be in a bad mood. What she was not aware of, however, was how she judged and condemned him—at least one time every 30 seconds, and sometimes more. Since she could not perceive this I decided to videotape their session. Then we would review it together. The session went just as I had expected. She condemned and attacked him at least a dozen times in five minutes. However, as we watched this session rerun on the videotape, she became upset—at him! She was upset at him for acting so terribly and she wasn't too pleased with me either for the whole idea. With all the prompting she could not see herself interacting negatively. She could not allow herself to get the log out of her own eye.

Judgmentalism can also serve another function. If you are frightened by closeness in a relationship, judgmentalism serves the vital function of keeping distance in the relationship. Some people grow up in families where, if they get close, they are either consumed by the parent or are hurt. For them it is safer to keep distance. By constantly judging their spouse or children, they keep what to them is a safety zone of distance.

I suppose that one could argue that Christ did make judgments about the Pharisees; however, I think that we also have to remember that He was Christ. His function, motivation, understanding and purpose are significantly different from the rest of us.

We are called into openness with others, not separation that is caused by judgment. Love cannot be well-expressed in an atmosphere of judgment.

Questions for Discussion

1. How do you respond when you feel judged?

2. What is our obligation to other people in terms of changes in their lives, styles of relating or behaving?

3. What does it mean that we will be judged in the same way that we judge others?

4. What causes some people to be more actively judgmental of others?

5. How does judgmentalism affect relationships within your own family?

6. Of the people you know in whose lives you've seen change, what caused them to change?

Matthew 7:12

Therefore, whatever you want men to do to you, you also do to them, for this is the [meaning of the] Law and the Prophets.

Summary of Principles of Relationships

1. When angry don't treat the person you're angry with as worthless.
2. When threatened don't refuse to be reconciled.
3. Don't use others, even in your thoughts.
4. Do not return hurt to those who have hurt you.
5. If taken advantage of, give even more.
6. If forced to do something, do even more.
7. If you are asked for something, give it to the person.
8. If someone wants to borrow something, loan it to him.
9. Love those who seek to hurt you.
10. Don't seek to impress others, but do your loving actions in secret.
11. Forgive those who have offended you.
12. Utilize your days building others up, not accumulating possessions.
13. Do not judge others for their faults.
14. Treat others the way you want to be treated.

16

The "Golden-Rule" Life

Matthew 7:12

"Do for others what you would have them do for you."

Perhaps Matthew 7:12 summarizes the whole set of principles that Christ has been teaching. I hear Him saying, "Think about how you would like to be treated and go and do that to others." What we once called "The Golden Rule" we now call "empathy." It encourages us to put ourselves into someone else's shoes. We are encouraged to think about how the world looks to the other. It helps us to better understand how to treat others when we filter our view through how we would like to be treated. If we had grown up in the circumstances in which they did, we might be just like them.

What basic needs do you have that you would like others to meet? A need for love and respect? To not have to perform in order to be accepted? Space to attempt and fail and still be accepted? Freedom to be yourself and not have to please somebody else? Freedom to not always have to be pleasant or nice? Not having to feel "compared" or "inferior"?

What would your family be like if you applied these principles? How well do you think you are doing with your spouse and children? Your mother, father, your in-laws? Are you treating them in a way that you would like to be treated? What can you do to improve your relationships? What steps can you take to grow?

It is common for people to want a success formula for life. These principles from Matthew are not meant as a series of rules to live by in order to have a successful life. "It is the letter of the law that kills, but the Spirit gives life" (see 2 Cor. 3:6). If these principles become laws, they will not help one's family life; they will only cause guilt, self-pressure and struggle.

It is interesting to note that in the last half of Matthew 7:12 Christ says, This is the meaning of the whole law of Moses. All of those rules and regulations in the law are designed to lead one to this very conclusion: "Do unto others as you would have them do unto you." All of those rules were not there for the sake of having rules; they were there because (as the ad says) they are good for you. They were there to lead people into a more Christ-like relationship with one another. Yet people took the laws that were designed to bring love into relationships and used them to beat each other over the head. Sometimes they even use them to beat themselves over the head. If these principles which Christ taught about relating simply become the "Mosaic Law" of the New Testament, they likewise will kill the spirit of people.

Through the power of the Holy Spirit we can learn to live in the Kingdom of God. We can become free and can express the abundancy Christ spoke about. Here Christ is saying, "Here it is. When you live in my Spirit and follow me you will look like this." It is a matter of letting go of our human nature and gaining His nature. It seems to me that in many ways these principles involve people going against the rushing current of self-acquisition and self-preservation.

In essence the principles teach us that we should be willing to "let go." The lives that many people live involve a program of accumulation—accumulation of recognition, skills, money, prestige, friends, power, control over others, etc. Yet these principles from Matthew apparently are stating that life in the Kingdom is a process of letting go or releasing. Let go of judging others; let go of power over others; let go of possessions when others have need of them; let go of punishing enemies; let go of returning evil; let go when people force you to go that extra mile. By not letting go, perhaps people take upon themselves the job of caring for themselves rather than letting God care for them.

Christ seems to be saying, however, that the way to freedom as a person and having life abundantly is the opposite of that which we do. Freedom comes from being able to let go, not control. I see this same principle manifested day after day through couples with whom I talk. When they place expectations on each other, their next step is to force, control or manipulate the other into doing what they want them to do. If you think about all of the conflicts you have had, you'll see that they are related in some way to trying to get someone else to do what you want him to do. When you cannot let go of others, pressure builds in the relationship. There is a necessity for expressing needs to others, but then it is important to realize that if they never do what you want, it still will not ruin your happiness in life. Those couples who are able to let go and move on in life are also the ones who seem the most content and happy.

I think that in many ways God has designed all of life to be a process of letting go, not a process of acquiring. Eventually, by design, you are asked to let go of life itself. However, one lets go in order to gain a new life that is even more fulfilling. In the same way that a grain of wheat cannot produce until it falls into the ground and dies, so you cannot gain new life until you let go of self.

When you treat others the way you want to be treated, it means being given the freedom to be yourself. Since Christ did this for you, it makes it possible for you to treat others the same way. I hope that considering these principles will develop a hunger in you to better know the mind of God. I also hope that as a result of knowing God's system of relating, the principles will seep like a fog into your own life as you grow up unto Him. "Do unto others as you would have them do unto you."

What Christ seems to be saying is, "Here are some principles for relating. I have come that you might have life and have it more abundantly. Do you want an enriched life, do you want a meaningful relationship with your husband, your wife or kids? Here are some principles that are related to the abundant life."

These principles are not meant to produce a Pollyanna life-style. However, in an age of pessimism about family life I must say that an enjoyable, meaningful, abundant life is possible. We can build relationships, we can enjoy each other, we can know a sense of fullness and richness in our families. Families do have strengths as a family unit on which meaningful times and adventures of life can be built and developed.

Ron had been slowly growing toward an awareness of Wendy's style of relating over the years. The more he understood her the easier it was to relate and the more he enjoyed their relationship. He saw with eyes of understanding now, whereas before he had seen only her behavior. Their growth had really started in earnest four or five years ago. It was at that point Ron had taken some action on a decision he had been processing internally.

For several years he had prayed that he would know God and become more like Him in his relationships with others. From this desire and repeated prayer, God had brought a variety of unexpected people into his life, each one contributing something more to his understanding of God. He realized the centrality in the Bible of God's desire for relationship to mankind and man's unreliability in that relationship as he strives to live in autonomy and self-sufficiency. He began studying the New Testament to determine how Christ related and what He taught about relationships. He prayed for the power to live the life that he saw as a potential.

Things began changing for Ron. As he became aware of the way he related to God, it didn't bother him so much when Wendy let him down. He became aware of how important relationships are in all of life's experiences. He actually tried living the Sermon on the Mount. Others began noticing their family life. Some wondered about it, others questioned. He and Wendy knew, however, what was happening between them. She became more open about her feelings; she revealed more of herself as the trust and understanding grew between them. As a couple they increased their admiration and respect for each other. Their kids began to respond to some of the changes and soon the whole family was growing as a unit. They were now free to reach out to others.

In looking back they realized that the pivotal point had been their desire to know God better and to seek His power to model their lives after Jesus. Many friends appreciated and drew strength from the changes they saw. A few dismissed their strength by labeling it as "they got their act together." What Ron and Wendy have achieved is not a secret impossibility. It is a process that is available to many who are willing to seek it. The journey toward living in the Kingdom may be very different for each person, but the destination is the same.

Questions for Discussion

1. For what reason or intention should you do to others as you would have them do to you?

2. In what ways does the world look different through different people's eyes?

3. What do we need to know about a person in order to treat him in the way he would like to be treated?

4. How do your family members want to be treated?

5. How do you want to be treated by other family members? Are there any specific changes that you would like from any specific family member?

6. What would be the most difficult part (for you personally) of living a Kingdom life?

7. How do you think you would feel about living out the principles from the Sermon on the Mount?

Other Regal Books
to help you build
better relationships: